Controlling
the Fires of

Anger

DR. LINDSEY GARMON

21ST CENTURY CHRISTIAN

Cover design by Martell Speigner

ISBN: 978-0-89098-367-6

Table of Contents

Introduction

Fire and Anger—Why the Connection?

Have you thought about our anger-related terminology? There is a lot of heat and fire symbolism contained in it. Clearly, we tend to connect anger with fire-related words, ideas, and experiences. After watching and listening to angry people, and experiencing the emotion within our own lives, we have learned that anger is frequently "hot"—fire-like. So, when speaking of "angry people," "angry feelings," and "angry situations," we make reference to...

...*hot* tempers

...being *boiling mad*

...blowing off *steam*

...*blistering* comments

...*scorching* remarks

...*heated* arguments

...having *a short fuse*

...*volatile* situations

...being *hot under the collar*

...*smoldering* resentments

...*seething* frustrations

...*sparking* controversy

...emotional *meltdowns*

...having *fire in our eyes*

...*igniting* arguments

...*losing our cool*

...being *hotheaded*

...*explosive* issues
...*fiery* personalities
...*exploding with anger*
...*blazing* words
...*blowing* up
...*burning* anger

Fire Is Hot—And So Is Uncontrolled Anger

Obviously, we do make connections between fire and anger. Why? Because when we are angry, there is a tendency to seethe, ignite, explode, and burn emotionally. In a number of ways, anger is like fire. It can be helpful or it can be harmful. It can serve constructive purposes if properly controlled or it can be extremely destructive and deadly if it rages out of control. Just as physical fire can so quickly burn, scar, damage, and kill, anger can cause ugly emotional scars, damage the human spirit, and even leave emotional, relational, spiritual, and physical death in its destructive path. Fire is hot—and so is uncontrolled anger!

Do not make friends with a hot-tempered man, do not associate with one easily angered, or you may learn his ways and get yourself ensnared. (Proverbs 22:24-25)

My dear brothers, take note of this: Everyone should be quick to listen, slow to speak and slow to become angry, for man's anger does not bring about the righteous life that God desires. (James 1:19-20)

So...Be Careful With Fire—And Anger!

It's a rather simple concept—this analogy between "fire" and "anger." Because anger has many fire-like characteristics and effects, we need to respect and treat anger as we do fire. Why do we use such caution when we are dealing with even the smallest flame of fire? Because we understand its volatile nature as well as the pain and destruction it can cause. Being careful with physical fire keeps us from injuring other people as well as ourselves. A similar respect for anger and its potential effects will keep us from blistering and burning others with the fires of anger.

Making this connection between "fire" and "anger," we are now ready to enter into a study that will demonstrate how principles related to "fire-safety" can be adapted spiritually to insure that we live in a daily environment that insures "anger safety." The objective will be to learn how legitimate anger can be expressed to the right people, in the right way, at the right time, and to the right degree so that God is honored, people are helped, and we are strengthened.

In your anger do not sin: Do not let the sun go down while you are still angry, and do not give the devil a foothold. (Ephesians 4:26-27)

Chapter 1

The Capacity For Anger—Who?

Anger—What Is It?

Anger is completely normal and can be healthy. A certain amount of anger is necessary to our survival. It exists in varying degrees all the way from a mild irritation to a raging fury. Anger is our instinctive emotional response when we deal with many of life's frustrations, disappointments, injustices, hurts, insults, or losses. It is that feeling of being put out or outraged when what we experience does not match what we expect or need. The painful truth is that much of our anger is rooted in the fact that we do not get our way!

Consider these stages or levels of anger:

Level 1: Frustration

Frustration is that internal feeling of displeasure and discomfort over unwanted conditions and circumstances. Your frustration level must be carefully monitored because if it continues to rise, it can become the spark that ignites a flame of resentment.

Level 2: Resentment

Resentment is mental displeasure that keeps on churning and burning within us. The irritation continues. The undesirable conditions remain. The mental tapes get replayed again and again. This creates a mindset that is potentially volatile. If the situation is not resolved in due time, the flame of resentment can quickly be fanned into a blaze of indignation.

Level 3: Indignation

Indignation is anger that is full-blown. At this level, honesty calls for a person to truthfully say, "I am angry!" Anger has effects on your body, mind, and spirit. Indignation frequently stirs a natural desire to correct, punish, or get revenge. At this point, your anger may be expressed in healthy or unhealthy ways. If the fires of indignation are not controlled quickly and effectively, they can become a blaze of rage or an inferno of fury.

Level 4: Rage Or Fury

Rage or fury is anger that is totally out of control. Such fits of ugly anger can appear to others as a state of emotional and mental madness. At this level, anger is always sinful and destructive.

Do you see the steady progression in these levels of anger? Some people live at one of these levels continually. They carry a chip on both shoulders and walk around as human time bombs just ready to "go off" at the least provocation. The quick-tempered person can move from the spark of frustration to an inferno of rage in a fraction of a second. Such anger is always dangerous, damaging, and sinful!

At What Point Does Our Anger Become Sinful?

When does anger that is not sinful become anger that is sinful? Where is the line of demarcation? And, when do we cross it? Only God can know the human heart and accurately make such determinations.

Anger in any stage and at any level is dangerous and should be controlled with prayer and care. Certainly, anytime an individual's wrath reaches a point where it is out of control, the line of sinfulness has been crossed. The Christian's challenge is to learn the spiritual discipline of practicing a healthy anger that is aroused for the right reasons, displayed in the right manner, embraced for the right length of time, and ultimately resolved according to biblical principles.

Do not assume that all sinful anger surfaces as heated rage and fury. The fires of sinful anger can burn quietly beneath the surface, yet still be damaging and deadly. So-called hidden anger results in passive-aggressive behaviors such as pouting, contrariness, hidden bitterness, or even hatred. While appearing cool on the surface, these forms of anger are just as dangerous, hurtful, and sinful as expressions of rage and fury.

Deal With Anger Quickly!

One of the keys to controlling the fires of anger is to deal with it aggressively as soon as possible. Every second counts once the spark of frustration appears or the flame of resentment burns. While it may not be easy to pinpoint the precise moment at which legitimate anger becomes sinful anger, most of us have crossed that line and experienced the remorse and guilt that comes. Anger changes your body chemistry. It creates a disturbing mindset. It stirs all sorts of negative emotions. It has a way of draining and depleting your spiritual strength. It even affects your countenance. When anger rages, everything changes!

Anger Control Exercise 1

1. Based on your personal experiences with anger, how far up the "anger-scale" mentioned above have you moved? Place an "X" on the lines to indicate the anger-levels you have personally experienced.

    _____ I have experienced the *"rage"* and *"fury"* level of anger.

    _____ I have experienced the *"indignation"* level of anger.

    _____ I have experienced the *"resentment"* level of anger.

    _____ I have experienced the *"frustration"* level of anger.

2. Read *Galatians 5:19-21, Ephesians 4:31-32, Colossians 3:8-10, and Luke 15:25-32.* Identify the words, phrases, or behaviors appearing in these passages that are anger-related.

3. At what point on the anger scale are you most likely to feel uncomfortable and unhappy? At what point do you notice changes occurring within your body? At what point are you most likely to sin with your tongue?

4. Why is it so crucial for us to deal with anger early and aggressively? Even though we know, intellectually, this is the right thing to do, why is it difficult to carry out?

Anger Is Part Of Being Human

The spark of anger is alive, to some degree, within the spirit of every healthy human being. Think of it as a small glowing ember that resides within the nature of every person from the time of birth. We come "from the factory" with a capacity for anger.

So many things can aggravate and cause us to feel angry. We get angry with our marriage mates and children, friends and strangers, bosses and employees, utility companies and government bureaucracies, the world's injustices—even the price of a gallon of gasoline or telemarketers who call repeatedly. Such realities are the inescapable irritations of life. Sometimes the feeling of anger is one of mild agitation and is quickly dismissed. At other times, it can be long lasting and hard to manage. The question is not, "Will you get angry?" The question is, "When and where will you get angry and how will you control it?"

Anger Control Exercise 2

1. Imagine yourself as a Christian counselor. Your Christian client says, "My goal is to eliminate all anger from my life. I want to reach a level of emotional and spiritual maturity that will allow me to live completely anger-free!" Would this be a realistic or desirable goal for your client? As a counselor, how would you respond to such a

request? What words of wisdom would you share?

2. Do you agree with the observation, "Anger is a part of being human?" How could this observation be misused and abused?

3. In what sense could Christians have an unhealthy fear of anger?

The Capacity For Anger Is God-Given And God-Like

Our Creator has wired and equipped us with the ability to feel irritation and aggravation—to get angry. The Bible says, ***"Be angry...****and sin not!"* (Ephesians 4:26 KJV, RSV) In fact, the capacity for righteous anger makes us like God.

> *God is a righteous judge, a God who expresses his wrath every day. (Psalm 7:11)*

> *The LORD is compassionate and gracious, slow to anger, abounding in love. (Psalm 103:8)*

> *For forty years, I (God) was angry with that generation; I said, "They are a people whose hearts go astray, and they have not known my ways." So I have declared on oath in my anger, "They shall never enter my rest." (Psalm 95:10-11)*

> *The wrath of God is being revealed from heaven against all the god-lessness and wickedness of men who suppress the truth by their wickedness...(Romans 1:18)*

Obviously, the Bible does not hesitate to assign angry feelings to God. The inspired writers never shied away from the fact that we serve a loving God who, at times, gets angry. He is not indifferent to or unaffected by the selfish attitudes and wicked actions of his creatures. The God who loves so tenderly is the same God who can express his anger so intensely. Our God understands anger.

Because we are created in the image of our God, we, too, will inevitably experience feelings of anger. *(Genesis 1:26-27)* Like our ability to think and make decisions, our ability to feel anger is from God.

God's Anger And Ours—There Is A Difference

Even though the Bible uses the same words to describe divine and human anger, we should understand that there are striking differences between the two.

First, God's anger is always morally justified and properly motivated. *(Genesis 6:5-7, 11-13)* Human anger is not. Frequently, we get angry for the wrong reasons.

Second, unlike human anger, God's wrath is not easily provoked. Frequently, the message of the Bible is, *"God is slow to anger." (Psalm 145:8)* In contrast, some of us tend to get angry easily and quickly.

Third, the wrath of God never contradicts or cancels out His loving nature. In every case, His love and His wrath can stand side by side. God's righteous anger keeps His love from becoming a shallow sentimentality that is complacent and indulgent *(Jonah 3:1-10)*. Too often, our anger-episodes have absolutely no connection with a genuine love for God or others. Instead, they tend to reflect a love of self.

Anger Control Exercise 3

1. During the days of Noah, God sent a flood upon the earth. This is one example of "divine wrath." Can you cite two additional examples of "God's wrath" that are mentioned in the Scriptures?

2. How can God display His wrath, yet not forfeit His loving nature? The Bible says, "God is love." *(1 John 4:8)* How can he be "love" and at the

same time be "angry?" What is the practical implication of this fact?

3. Do you agree or disagree that the ability to feel anger is part of what it means *"To be created in the image of God"*? Explain.

4. Why do you suppose it makes some people uncomfortable to refer to God as being "angry"? Explain.

5. In our feeble efforts to understand God's divine nature, how would you compare the importance of knowing "God's wrath" with that of knowing "his love"? *(Romans 11:22)*

How Far Back Can We Trace Sinful Anger?

Anger has been around for a long time. We can trace it back to the first family and the horrible incident that occurred just outside the Garden of Eden. It involved the two sons of Adam and Eve—Cain and Abel.

> *Adam lay with his wife Eve and she became pregnant and gave birth to Cain. She said, "With the help of the LORD I have brought forth a man." Later she gave birth to his brother Abel. Now Abel kept flocks, and Cain worked the soil.*
>
> *In the course of time Cain brought some of the fruits of the soil as an offering to the LORD. But Abel brought fat portions from some of the firstborn of his flock. The LORD looked with favor on Abel and his offering, but on Cain and his offering he did not look with favor.*
>
> *So Cain was very angry, and his face was downcast. Then the LORD said to Cain, "Why are you angry? Why is your face downcast? If you do what is right, will you not be accepted? But if you do not do what is right, sin is crouching at your door; it desires to have you, but you must master it."*

Now Cain said to his brother Abel, "Let's go out to the field." And while they were in the field, Cain attacked his brother Abel and killed him.

Then the LORD said to Cain, "Where is your brother Abel?" "I don't know," he replied. "Am I my brother's keeper?" The LORD said, "What have you done? Listen! Your brother's blood cries out to me from the ground. Now you are under a curse and driven from the ground, which opened its mouth to receive your brother's blood from your hand. When you work the ground, it will no longer yield its crops for you. You will be a restless wanderer on the earth."

Cain said to the LORD, "My punishment is more than I can bear. Today you are driving me from the land, and I will be hidden from your presence; I will be a restless wanderer on the earth, and whoever finds me will kill me." (Genesis 4:1-14)

Anger Control Exercise 4

1. Before Cain felt the intense anger that led him to murder his brother, Abel, what thoughts and feelings do you think he was having? What were the "primary emotions" that first stirred within him, which then triggered the "secondary emotion" of anger?

2. Read *Genesis 37:3-11*. What do you think were the "primary emotions" that Joseph's brothers were feeling before they grew to hate him and then sell him into slavery?

3. Why is it important for us to understand "primary" and "secondary" emotions as we seek to control our anger?

You Will Get Angry

We don't control whether or not we will get angry. We will! The capacity for anger is standard equipment for humans. Place it right alongside the ability to laugh or cry—the ability to get angry is God-given.

What we can and must control is the manner in which we manage our anger. A determination never to get angry simply causes us to internalize the problem so instead of a red face or red ears on the outside, we get artery blockages on the inside. There is simply no cure for anger if by "cure" you mean eradicating all causes and sources of frustration in the world. There's always something to aggravate or irritate. Even in the Bible, godly people are described as those who dealt constructively with anger rather than people who never got angry.

Anger Control Exercise 5

1. In view of the content of this lesson, would you agree or disagree with the statement that "the capacity to express healthy and legitimate anger is a part of God's ideal design for humans?" Explain.

Helpful Insights From This Chapter To Remember And Use...

1.

2.

3.

4.

Chapter 2

Good Anger...Bad Anger—Which?

Not All Fires Are the Same

In the chill of winter, there's nothing quite like relaxing in front of a toasty fire. It can sure take the edge off a busy day. Sharing the firelight with loved ones makes the experience even better. For many, this is a peaceful dreamland. The smell is aromatic. The warmth imparts a feeling of well-being. The scene and sound inspire cozy feelings. Yes, there's fire within the house, but the flames are burning in the right place, under controlled circumstances, and providing wonderful benefits for those who are gathered near. The fire hurts no one. No damage. No scars. In fact, everybody's helped. This is "good fire."

This tranquil scene can change drastically and suddenly. This peaceful, fireside dreamland can turn into a horrible and volatile nightmare. A hidden creosote build-up in the chimney can ignite and cause raging fire to spread to other parts of the house. What was once under control and constructive is now out of control and destructive. People burned, valuable property destroyed, irreplaceable items gone forever, or even lives lost. This is "bad fire."

Fire has been a helpful friend to the human family for centuries. When used properly, it has enabled us to eliminate bad things and construct good things. Controlled fires provide warmth or even the means for survival in the midst of cold and hostile environments. In many ways, fire is a positive force of energy. However, when it gets out of control, fire becomes a deadly instrument of pain and destruction.

Not All Anger Is The Same

Like fire, there is "good anger" and there is "bad anger." Yes, you read correctly. There is "good anger."

The fires of righteous anger can be fanned into a flame that can provide light in the midst of dark places and courage in the midst of scary places. When the glowing ember of anger within the human spirit is properly managed, it becomes a resource for the elimination of evil and the preservation of good. Some of the most repulsive physical, social, and spiritual ills that have plagued humanity have been eliminated because somebody got angry. When mothers who had lost children to drunk drivers exercised their legitimate wrath, the organization, Mothers Against Drunk Drivers (MADD), was created. No doubt, thousands of lives have been saved because a few moms got angry! Just one person who is justifiably angry can make an enormous impact on the world. Controlled anger is necessary to the establishment and maintenance of social order and civic life. The world needs more good anger.

However, if the glowing ember of anger is fanned into a blaze that leads to bitterness, hatred, grudges, division, violence, or rage, the results are always damaging and deadly to the perpetrator and dangerous to everyone else who has proximity. Even a silent, seething type of anger—concealed anger—can cause deep hurt to those who are the objects of our wrath. Sinful anger is bad anger!

Do What The Bible Says—*"Be Angry..." (Ephesians 4:26 KJV)*

There are times when we should be angry! Sometimes it's wrong to be anything but angry.

Three "P-words" help us to remember the circumstances and conditions when "good anger" is appropriate.

1. When *"P-eople"* are being abused and shamefully treated, the proper kind of anger is justified.

2. When **"P-rinciples"** of God's truth are being rebelliously ignored or proudly exploited and violated, legitimate anger is in order.
3. Or, when **"P-eace"** is being destroyed by perpetrators who hold selfish and sinful agendas, righteous anger is the proper response.

In the face of such evils, it is wrong to passively retreat and fail to demonstrate justified anger. In such instances, righteous indignation is a godly trait. This is "good anger."

Too Much Of Our Anger Is "Bad Anger"

Sadly, much of our anger is not "righteous anger." Even when it starts out as righteous indignation, it can so quickly turn selfish, savage, and sinful. Religious radicals blaze with anger. Anger is behind terrorism and hate crimes. It drives bloody civil conflicts and wars. Watch the six o'clock news. Read the newspaper. Drive the freeways. Walk the fairways. Listen to the airwaves. Observe what is happening in the workplace. Monitor what is going on within the home place. Anger levels seem to be elevated. More people seem to be angry and on-edge than ever before. C. Leslie Charles, author of *Why Is Everyone So Cranky?* writes, "Rage is the rage today."

Mess up our order, delay our flight, fail to move immediately when the light turns green, cut in on us in traffic and—BOOM—we erupt! The general culture has accommodated higher and higher levels of anger without many objecting or even noticing. The societal guideline used to be "keep the lid on." Too often today, the tendency is to "take the lid off."

Anger Control Exercise 1

In the three passages listed below, you will read about situations where some form of righteous anger—good anger—is being displayed or expressed. To the right of each passage, there is an **"A," "B," and "C."** After you read each passage, considering the context and circumstances being described, circle the letter or letters that explain why the anger being expressed was "good anger." (Circle more than one letter in each case if multiple abuses were occurring.) If you are studying with a group, discuss the reasons for your answers.

If *"P-eople"* were being sinfully abused and hurt, circle the **"A"**

If *"P-rinciples"* of God's Truth were being violated, circle the **"B"**

If *"P-eace"* between people was being selfishly disrupted, circle the **"C"**

1. *Matthew 23:1-3, 15* .. **A   B   C**

2. *Romans 16:17-18* ... **A   B   C**

3. *Galatians 2:11-14* .... **A   B   C**

How Could Anger Ever Be Good?

Some people are surprised to discover that anger, under any circumstances, is ever justifiable. So much of what we think and feel related to anger is rooted in our childhood perceptions and memories. It is not uncommon to find individuals who grew up in Christian families where anger was always labeled as a sinful act. In some cases, this message was explicit. In other families, it was implicit. People who have authority in the lives of young children can leave the impression that a "good child" never gets angry—the child who "stuffs" her anger is rewarded, while the one who "spews" his anger is punished. These messages get through to children and have an impact on them in adulthood.

We may have grown up in home settings where ugly displays of uncontrolled anger were frequent, which translated into hurt, alienation, or violence within our families of origin. Thus, whether we were taught that anger is wrong or surmised the same based on painful experiences, the bottom line is that some still embrace the view that all anger should be avoided. Nice people don't get angry and Christians are nice people.

Thus, there are conscientious followers of Christ who operate on the assumption that if one is truly led by the Spirit of God, he or she will never be angry. Anger is treated like a forbidden emotion. Thinking that anger is sinful, these individuals will go to great lengths to avoid admitting anger. They will claim to be uptight, upset, ticked, irked, annoyed, troubled, perturbed, disgusted, cross, aggravated, peeved, griped, grumpy, or hurt, but will not say, "I am angry!"

Anger Control Exercise 2

1. Within the setting where you were reared as a child, was it as acceptable to say, "I am angry!" as it was to say, "I am hungry!" How did those in charge (parents or church leaders) view the emotion of anger?

2. Can you identify a personal experience in which you demonstrated "good anger"? How did this feel? How did you behave as you expressed your anger? What was the outcome? What were "the keys" that prevented "good anger" from becoming "bad anger"?

3. Painful as it may be, would you be willing to identify a situation in your life where you expressed "sinful anger"? How did this feel? What was the outcome? What could you have done differently to prevent the outburst of "bad anger"?

4. When you express "sinful anger," how does it tend to affect your body?

5. When you express "sinful anger," how does it tend to affect your mind and spirit?
6. When you express "sinful anger," how are the people around you usually affected?
7. In the chapter, reference was made to the work of MADD (Mothers Against Drunk Drivers). Can you think of other organizations or causes that illustrate the benefits of "good anger"?
8. In what sense is the church to exercise righteous anger as it serves God in the midst of a sinful culture?

Jesus Got Angry—But He Did Not Sin

Jesus was no "emotionless person." (When you think about it, those two words are mutually exclusive.) There are people who will accept a partially emotional Jesus, but not a Lord who experienced the full range of human emotions like ours. Of course, everybody accepts the fact that He freely expressed love and joy. A few seem to struggle with the idea that He had a healthy sense of humor. But, many more seem to resist the idea that Jesus actually got...ANGRY. In their effort to deny that Jesus became angry, they say He experienced "a divine jealousy"—not anger. "But He was sinless! How could He have gotten angry?" they say.

The Son of God did experience righteous anger—"good anger"! In each instance, He vented His displeasure for the right reasons, to the right people, in the right way, at the right time, and to the right degree. Yes, He was angry, but in His anger, He never sinned.

When He saw religious shysters making a killing in the Temple courts—His Father's house—at the expense of the poor, He was angry and He took appropriate action right on the scene. In fact, it appears that Jesus took bold action to cleanse the Temple on two separate occasions—early in His ministry (John 2:13-17) and during the final week before His crucifixion (Matthew 21:12-13; Mark 11:12-19; Luke 19:45-48).

In His first episode of Temple-cleansing, Jesus boldly moved into that sacred space and called a halt to what was going on. He made a whip out of cords, turned over money tables, and had animal fur and bird feathers flying. The Scriptures tell us *"he was consumed with zeal for his Father's House."* On this day, a legitimately angry Jesus was cleaning His Father's house!

> *When it was almost time for the Jewish Passover, Jesus went up to Jerusalem. In the temple courts he found men selling cattle, sheep and doves, and others sitting at tables exchanging money. So he made a whip out of cords, and drove all from the temple area, both sheep and cattle; he scattered the coins of the moneychangers and overturned their tables. To those who sold doves he said, "Get these out of here! How dare you turn my Father's house into a market!" His disciples remembered that it is written: "Zeal for your house will consume me." (John 2:12-17)*

On another occasion, when self-righteous religious people complained and condemned because Jesus healed a man with a shriveled hand, He was angry at the sight of their shriveled hearts. The gospel writer Mark describes the scene.

> *Another time he went into the synagogue, and a man with a shriveled hand was there. Some of them were looking for a reason to accuse Jesus, so they watched him closely to see if he would heal him on the Sabbath. Jesus said to the man with the shriveled hand, "Stand up in front of everyone." Then Jesus asked them, "Which is lawful on the Sabbath: to do good or to do evil, to save life or to kill?" But they remained silent. He looked around at them in anger and, deeply distressed at their stubborn hearts, said to the man, "Stretch out your hand." He stretched it out, and his hand was completely restored. Then the Pharisees went out and began to plot with the Herodians how they might kill Jesus. (Mark 3:1-6)*

Anger Control Exercise 3

1. Read Mark's account of Jesus making His triumphal entry into Jerusalem and then cleansing the Temple—*Mark 11:1-19*. In this account, Mark records an important detail about Jesus' behavior that confirms the fact that even though He was very displeased with the conditions He saw in the Temple area, He exercised total control over His anger. Can you pinpoint this important detail in Mark's gospel?

2. In *Matthew 23*, there is an example of Jesus' righteous indignation toward the hypocrisy and legalism of the religious leaders of His day. As you read this chapter, identify three statements made by Jesus which illustrate His righteous anger toward their sin.

Helpful Insights From This Chapter To Remember And Use...

1.

2.

3.

4.

Chapter 3

Anger Inspection—Willing?

Firefighters Call It Being "Fire-Wise"

Professional firefighters continually stress the importance of regular fire inspections. Their objective is to find hazards that may cause fire or impede escape in the event of a fire. They look for faulty wiring, overloaded circuits, combustible substances, potential dangers in the cooking area, and problems with fire extinguishers, sprinkler systems, or other fire safety equipment. In the event of a fire, they want to do everything possible to ensure a successful escape.

With critical eyes, fire inspectors pay close attention to details and conditions that might start or encourage the spread of fire. They are eager to promote fire prevention, fire suppression, and proper fire use. These helpful professionals are relentless in their efforts to prevent fire from causing injury, loss of life, and property. Concerned firefighters always prefer to ask, "What can we do to prevent the fire?" rather than, "What must we do to put the fire out?"

Anger-Fighters Must Be "Anger-Wise"

In our efforts to prevent bad anger and control good anger, we must become "anger-wise." Anger prevention is our first line of defense. As George Bailey once said it, "It is better to prepare and prevent than to repair and repent." The better we understand our own unique "anger patterns," the more likely we can avoid sin caused by anger. This calls for a close and careful "anger inspection"—the kind that requires a thorough inspection of the depths of the heart. Are you willing?

"Anger-Denial" Blocks The Way To "Anger-Wisdom"

We all know what it means to say that a person is "in denial." An alcoholic can say to the world and to himself, "I don't have a problem and I can quit any time I want to." Yet, he continues to drink and refuses to face the impact of his drinking on himself and others around him. Denial is a common practice by which we avoid an uncomfortable or unacceptable self-awareness.

Are there times and situations when you lose control of your temper? When the fire of anger burns within you, are things said and done that are offensive to God and potentially hurtful to your family, friends, or co-workers?

Or, do you tend to sit on your anger? Some mistakenly believe that because they do not pitch fits that they do not have an anger problem. The truth is that silent, seething, buried anger can be just as destructive and sinful as anger that is vented in a fit of rage.

For those who are serious about controlling and expressing anger in a Christ-like manner, there is an important first step. That is to face our anger issues honestly, openly, and courageously with as little denial as possible.

Let's Do An "Anger Inspection"

Do you think you have a problem with anger? The self-test that follows is designed to help you make this determination by prompting you to take a close-up look at some of ways you are responding to the stressors of life and coping with your anger. The questions are for your own self-awareness and no measurement scale is provided for rating your answers. At the end, you will be the judge of what your responses mean. A "right" answer is a truthful answer.

A good way to use this test is to work through it alone as a means of gaining self-understanding. An even better way to use it is to discuss your responses with a trusted friend or small group. The objective is to allow this test to help you assess the level, source, style, and target of your anger.

1. _____ Yes _____ No   I believe that I do have an anger problem—it is a serious problem that seems to occur frequently, resulting in sin against God and pain to others. There are times when my anger is "out of control."

2. _____ Yes _____ No   In most instances, my expressions of anger have been justified—people needlessly offended me and thus deserved the anger I vented on them.

3. _____ Yes _____ No   I tend to be a person who is tense and uptight a good bit of the time.

4. _____ Yes _____ No   In many cases, I tend to be a person who does not say what is really on my mind—I tend to suppress my true feelings.

5. _____ Yes _____ No   Most of the time, I am able to control my anger. However, I do admit that there are situations where my anger leads to sin.

6. _____ Yes _____ No   Controlling anger is not a problem for me. I do get angry, but I do not sin in my angry moments.

7. _____ Yes _____ No   There are those times when, in anger, I speak words that are sinful and hurtful.

8. _____ Yes _____ No   I feel that sinful anger has, at times, caused damage to my physical health.

9. _____ Yes _____ No   There are people in my life who are hurt and scarred due to sinful anger that I have expressed.

10. _____ Yes _____ No   My anger is the "brooding type"—prompting periods of silence, pouting, sulking, sleeping, bitterness, or other types of passive-aggressive behavior.

11. _____ Yes _____ No   My anger tends to be the type that "blows"! In such episodes, I have been known to

shout, attack, curse, throw, or become violent.

12. _____ Yes _____ No   My job puts me in a position to see, hear, and express angry feelings and words.

13. _____ Yes _____ No   I agree with the idea that anger is not always sinful—that there is "good anger" and "bad anger."

14. _____ Yes _____ No   Due to anger, I have experienced a noticeable reaction within my physical body.

15. _____ Yes _____ No   I was reared in a home where there were frequent outbursts of anger and rage.

16. _____ Yes _____ No   In my past, I can recall an incident where I lost a job because of anger.

17. _____ Yes _____ No   Anger, at times, has caused a problem in my marriage or home life.

18. _____ Yes _____ No   I have had a friend or loved one tell me that I have a problem with anger.

19. _____ Yes _____ No   I have had a counselor or therapist tell me that I have a problem with anger.

20. _____ Yes _____ No   I have often felt guilt, remorse, or shame because of my anger.

21. _____ Yes _____ No   I do take personal responsibility for my anger—I do not ever blame its presence or power on anyone else. The problem is not what others are doing. The problem is with me and the way I am choosing to express my anger.

22. _____ Yes _____ No   I nearly always know why I am angry. I know the aggravating conditions or persons in which my anger is rooted.

23. _____ Yes _____ No   I carry a sense of failure and guilt because I have tried previously to overcome sinful anger, but have failed.

24. _____ Yes _____ No | I freely admit that I am not strong enough to successfully deal with my anger problem. I need God's help as well as the help of other people.

25. _____ Yes _____ No | I am willing to allow God and my fellow believers in Christ to help me learn better ways of controlling my anger.

26. _____ Yes _____ No | This is my first time to be involved in an intensive and focused study of anger and anger control.

27. _____ Yes _____ No | This is my first time to be involved in a biblically focused study of anger and anger control.

28. _____ Yes _____ No | Even though I am not proud of it, there have been times when I have harbored resentment, bitterness, and anger for lingering periods of time.

29. _____ Yes _____ No | I am a willing and cheerful participant in this study of anger. This is a study that I desire to make.

30. _____ Yes _____ No | I have received or am receiving special treatment for the problem of anger—counseling, medication, or some other form of help.

31. _____ Yes _____ No | I want to participate in a learning process that may help to heal ugly wounds that have been caused by my sinful anger.

32. _____ Yes _____ No | I believe that a person can learn to control anger.

33. _____ Yes _____ No | I am ready to submit myself to God and principles of truth in the Bible as a means of finding help for my anger problem.

34. _____ Yes _____ No | I fully understand that overcoming sinful anger is going to require changes in my thinking and behavior.

35. _____ Yes _____ No There is hope for me! I can, with God's help and the support of others, learn *"to be angry and sin not."(Ephesians 4:26)*

Call It What It Is—Use The "A" Word

Go ahead. It's okay. Whether you experience "good anger" or "bad anger," you can and should call it what it is. You can say, "I am…ANGRY…and in my anger I am sinning." Or, you can say, "I am…ANGRY…but in my anger, I am not sinning." To name something is to acknowledge its existence. To name anger is to move beyond denial and take the first step toward assuming responsibility for it. It is essential to be honest about our anger. This is a necessary first step in learning to practice a healthy and holy anger.

Honest Confession Is Good

Where are you? Do the fires of sinful anger burn within your heart to any degree? Some people are angry and they declare it—honestly, openly.

No effort to conceal or cover it up. They can say, "Yes, I am mad! I am angry!"

Others are angry, but deny it. They call it by another name that sounds more socially acceptable. Consciously or unconsciously, they rationalize their sinful anger and find ways to justify it.

For some, intense anger is hidden away—presently concealed so that no one sees. This is a dangerous condition. The fires of anger can smolder in the deep recesses of the heart so that we, as well as others, remain oblivious to their deadly presence. Some are simply angry at life and have neither the means nor the motivation to deal with it properly.

Thankfully, there are some individuals who truly are free and clear of any trace of sinful anger. To cry "Anger-Fire!" in such cases would be to sound a false alarm. We must not cry "Fire!" when there is no anger. But neither must we live in denial of a hidden and repressed sinful anger that has the potential to cause great harm to others and ourselves.

Anger Control Exercise 1

1. Is it possible for a person to be very angry even though the anger is not seen or heard? Why is this a dangerous situation?
2. What benefits can you see to living in an environment where you can honestly and properly express your frustration and anger?

No Cover Ups—No Euphemisms

It's a fact. If the fires of anger are ever to be properly controlled or even extinguished, there must first be honest confession and open admission to God, to self, and to those with whom we are angry. We must come clean. Anger can never be properly controlled so long as it is covered up with euphemisms.

Name it! Yes, use the "**A**-word!"

Anger Control Exercise 2

How do you rate yourself? After working through the "Anger Inspection Exercise" given above and after prayerfully searching my own heart, I would rate my "anger-control performance" as…

_____ Successful and requiring no major change or improvement

_____ Moderately successful and needing slight improvement

_____ Deficient and needing significant improvement

_____ Seriously deficient and needing radical improvement

Helpful Insights From This Chapter To Remember And Use...

1.

2.

3.

4.

Secondary Causes of Anger—Be Aware!

Factors That May Contribute To Sinful Anger

Standing close to a blazing fire, you may not get burned, but you nearly always smell like smoke. Living in the midst of an angry culture can never be a justifiable cause of sinful anger, but it can expose us to conditions and circumstances that contribute to our struggles in this area. We can allow ourselves to be affected and infected by the angry climate around us.

In the midst of angry families, angry commuters, angry co-workers, angry political leaders, angry spectators, an angry media, angry religious fanatics, angry racial groups, and even angry churches, is it any wonder that the level of anger in our culture seems to be rising? Local and national news broadcasts are little more than daily "anger reports." We hear the gory details describing the actions of people who have acted out in anger since the previous broadcast. The following list highlights various conditions that may be contributing to our angry environment.

1. Cultural Dignity is Down

There is a general breakdown of good manners and social dignity within our culture. Rudeness and vulgarity are not only tolerated, but glorified. The TV talk shows are loud—opponents are yelling at each other. It's okay to say whatever is on your mind. Get it out! Inhibitions are gone. It is the spirit of our age, and it tends to give people permission to be loud, aggressive, or even angry. There is a sense that "anything goes." Just say it!

Anger Control Exercise I

1. In *I Corinthians 13:4-8,* Paul describes how love acts and reacts in a Christian's life. Which of the qualities in these verses is hardest for you to apply and practice when angry?
2. What Christian principles do you see in *Ephesians 4:29-5:2* that would greatly diminish the level of anger within your life?
3. From your vantage point, what three cultural trends are contributing to the rising level of anger in today's world?

2. A Sense of Entitlement is Exaggerated

Some say it. Many who don't say it, think it. "You owe me. I have rights. I want my freedom. I deserve my way." Feelings of entitlement! Fill a society with people who hold strong, even exaggerated feelings about what they deserve from others, and you are likely to find high levels of frustration and anger—even rage.

After all, who is favorably stroked in all the ways they desire? In this life, we soon learn that many things do not turn out the way we thought they would—our marriages, our children, our churches, our jobs, our country, and our world. Even God does not say, "Yes," to every request that we make of Him.

Anger is not a primary emotion—it is a secondary emotion. It kicks in after we first feel something else like hurt, disappointment, fear, embarrassment, frustration, or rejection. The most common trigger of anger is when we don't get our own way or when our expectations or perceived entitlements are not met. Unfulfilled expectations can stir anger.

Anger Control Exercise 2

1. Can you identify specific groups of people in today's culture who tend to act out in anger because they feel that their entitlements are being denied? In what way have unfulfilled expectations caused anger in your life?

2. As Christian parents, we have high hopes and expectations for our children. On the basis of the words in *Ephesians 6:4,* how could expectations become an "anger risk" for parents?

3. Can you identify an area of your life where high expectations may be setting you up for outbreaks of sinful anger?

3. Time Is Short

In all of our busyness, time is in short supply. Nobody has to ask the meaning of ASAP. There is nearly always a correlation between a shortage of time and a shortage of patience. Being rushed and being rude are, frequently, two sides of the same coin. Low levels of patience can lead to high levels of anger.

We're in a huge hurry. There are deadlines to meet and competition to beat. When we are in a rush and someone slows us down, we can so easily get agitated and angry. Feeling pressed and pushed by life's demands, we live at the edge of anger.

Anger Control Exercise 3

1. During a typical week, is there a particular time, place, or setting where you are most likely to feel tense and angry due to a shortage of time? What can you do to prevent this from becoming an opportunity for sinful anger to show itself in your life?

4. Daily Stressors Are Many

Our lives are crowded and crumpled up with stress. Demands are heavy. Office workers arrive to find dozens of e-mails that must be processed before they can start their business days. People feel the need to constantly multi-task in an effort to get it all done. It is common to have several jobs running on our computers at the same time. Stress becomes distress. Fatigue sets in. Exhaustion is a hallmark of the anger epidemic.

Anger Control Exercise 4

1. Life can have many stressors, but is there a specific area of your life that tends to be overloaded with "negative stressors"? Identify that area and then list two or three matters about which you need to pray in this regard.

2. Read *Luke 10:38-42*. Martha was upset with her sister—perhaps even with Jesus. What words in the text describe what was going on with Martha?

5. Life-Space Is Crowded

Ever feel crowded by people or surrounded by traffic? Are you feeling the need for some solitude? Overcrowding can stir feelings that spark the fires of anger. If you sit in traffic on freeways that have been clogged year after year, rage may seem rational. Parking lots are filled. Checkout lanes are long. Getting through security at the airport is a hassle. We feel frustrated and impatient.

How many of us have stood in the express line at the grocery store and counted the number of items in the cart of the person in front of us? When the feeling expressed by the words "Get out of my face" is what you are experiencing, you may be close to an emotional meltdown.

Anger Control Exercise 5

1. Is there a time or place when you are most likely to feel tense and irritable due to overcrowded conditions? How can such situations contribute to sinful anger in your experience?

6. A Desire to Control Is Engrained

Many of us learn early that anger is a tactic for gaining control and winning personal battles. We discover this as children in the checkout lane at the supermarket. Throw a screaming fit and guess what? You get your way.

These unhealthy "mad skills" carry over into adult situations at the office or at the negotiating table. The tactic may even work at home. Anger is powerful. Anger is energizing. It adds fire to our arguments. Some operate on the premise, "If I bark loudly and angrily enough, my opposition will back down!" Or, "If I pout and sulk long enough, I will get my way." This learned behavior can become an anger machine. Anger can be used as a weapon to get results.

Anger Control Exercise 6

1. Be very honest. Have you used sinful anger in any situation to get your way or to gain control? Describe the anger behavior you are most likely to display when you are feeling the need to control or manipulate.

7. Technology Is Intrusive

Technology can be a blessing that brings burdens. The world of high-tech can become intrusive. C. Leslie Charles says, "Cell phones, pagers, and other high tech devices allow us to be interrupted anywhere at anytime. On vacations, we carry the laptop and the demands of the job go with us. We are carrying the pressures of the workplace out on the highway as we transact business by phone. This constant accessibility, and compulsive use of technology fragments what little time we do have, adding to our sense of urgency, emergency, and overload."

Anger Control Exercise 7

1. Jesus was pressed by the demands of the crowds of people around Him. He made time to "get away" and be alone with His Father. *(Mark 1:32-35)* Do you feel that this is a need in your life? How is this need being met?
2. Does the technology of our day create irritations and anger struggles for you? How? What can you do to reduce these intrusions?

8. Wounds From the Past Are Deep

Confucius said, "To be wronged or robbed is nothing unless you remember it." Remembering our hurts over and over again is the essence of resentment. Grudges are rooted in the soil of resentment. When people deceive us, disappoint us, hurt us, and shatter our dreams, it is hard to forget and even harder to forgive. Old wounds that are not quickly and properly resolved can fester into emotional sores that spill bitterness into our lives.

Anger Control Exercise 8

1. Is there a conflict from your past that creates a lasting, seething kind of anger for you? What does the Lord want you to do to get this matter properly resolved?
2. How do the words of *Titus 3:3* apply in your situation? Share your victory over anger with others.

3. Read *James 3:13-18*. Make two columns on your paper. In the left column, write the words from the passage that describe "worldly wisdom." In the right column, write the words from the passage that describe the "wisdom from heaven." As you study the two columns, what observations and personal feelings come to mind as you think about your behavior?

9. Daily Life Is Highly Competitive

The workplace can be trying. Companies are downsizing. Competition is fierce. Good jobs are scarce. Bosses are demanding. Employees are disloyal. Colleagues are self-serving. Power struggles are going on. Customers are outraged. Forty or fifty hours a week in this environment tend to create a rumbling volcano that can suddenly erupt.

Anger Control Exercise 9

1. Why is it easy to become sinfully angry with our competitors?
2. Is there a competitor in your world who is especially difficult to deal with? Who? Why? How does this problem affect you?
3. What can you do to lessen the risk of becoming sinfully angry in this competitive situation of your life?

10. Relationships Are Tense

In too many marriages, there is lots of tension and turmoil. Spouses are fighting mad with each other. Homes are filled with headaches and heartaches as parents pull in one direction and kids pull in the other.

There's friction, which causes heat—chronic anger that can lead to abusive talk or even violence. Arguments escalate into shouting matches that threaten to "get physical." Frequently, the home setting is a powerful contributor to the overall anger-problem.

Anger Control Exercise 10

1. In the order of their intensity and potential danger, can you name the three relationships that are most likely to contribute to sinful anger in your daily life?
2. Focus on the relationship in your life that is most difficult for you. What can you do to lessen the risk of a sinful outbreak of anger?

Helpful Insights From This Chapter To Remember And Use...

1.

2.

3.

4.

Chapter 5

The Primary Cause of Anger—Beware!

Firefighters Look For Origin and Cause

We count on professional firefighters to rush to the scene of a fire and put their skills to good use. Their first priority is to save lives and extinguish the flames. Once the fire is put out, then fire investigators go about the important task of fulfilling priority number two—sifting through the aftermath of the blaze to determine its origin and cause. It is a process that gets repeated again and again. First, douse the fire. Then, determine its cause.

"Anger Fighters" Must Determine Origin And Cause

In contrast to the above, when fighting the fires of sinful anger, the process seems to work in reverse order. First, you must determine the origin and cause of the anger problem. Then, you must prayerfully deal with that cause by applying the appropriate Christian principles and disciplines so that a resolution is achieved as quickly as possible.

This is a crucial part of the "anger-fighting" process that enables you to douse or control the flames of your anger. The point is that frequently it is necessary to "get to the bottom of our anger"—determine why we are feeling the heat and hostility—before we can successfully "get on top of our anger." Yet, determining the origin and cause is sometimes difficult and oftentimes dangerously subjective.

At The Root Of All Bad Anger Is...SIN

Here's a fact that is painful, but very true. Every time the fires of sinful anger burn within a human life, the will of God is violated in some way and the heart of God, the Father, is broken. Thus, bad anger is serious because it is sinful! Could it be that we have made anger an "excusable sin?" Have we given ourselves permission to allow anger to go unresolved and unmanaged?

Blaming others for our anger is common. Rationalizing and excusing ourselves is typical. But, the hard fact remains, when anger burns out of control, you can know that sin has been committed in some way by someone. It may be that all parties involved in a situation may have had a part in the sinful act. Anger that is embraced and expressed sinfully is not okay. It is serious and it is sinful!

What Did Jesus Teach About Sinful Anger?

When Jesus walked on this earth, Jewish leaders had stressed the evil of murder, but had failed to stress the seriousness of anger. It must have been a shock to some when Jesus called for a change in emphasis. He called for His disciples to relate to people in a new and different way.

> *"You have heard that it was said to the people long ago, 'Do not murder, and anyone who murders will be subject to judgment.'*
> *But I tell you that anyone who is angry with his brother will be subject to judgment.*
> *Again, anyone who says to his brother, 'Raca,' is answerable to the Sanhedrin.*
> *But anyone who says, 'You fool!' will be in danger of the fire of hell."*
> (Matthew 5:21-22)

In these verses, Jesus points to three levels of anger where sin is involved. First, He cautions against unresolved anger toward a brother and points out that such an attitude in a Jewish community would be worthy of censure or judgment. This judgment could have been a "personal rebuke" that would come from a rabbi or local counsel of Jewish citizens. Anger was serious.

Second, Jesus refers to an anger that leads a person to resort to rude, offensive name-calling. *"Raca"* means "empty-headed"—the equivalent of calling someone an idiot. This practice in a Jewish community would call for a "judicial rebuke" by the Sanhedrin which was the highest court in the community. Obviously, Jesus did not view anger as something that was insignificant.

Third, He warns against a vicious anger that would relegate another person to the ranks of those who are fools and reprobates. This would be the equivalent of calling someone a moral fool and consigning the person to hell. Such deep-seated anger would cause one to be in danger of the fire of hell. This passage makes it clear that, to Jesus, sinful anger was never to be excused or taken lightly.

Other Key Passages That Reveal The Sinfulness Of Anger

In *Ephesians 4:27*, Paul says that sinful anger *"gives the devil a foothold in our lives."* In *verses 30-32*, he makes it clear that *"the Holy Spirit is grieved when bitterness, rage, or any forms of malice reside in the heart of a Christian believer."* Clearly, Paul is helping us to see that unmanaged anger is devilish—not divine.

This penetrating truth is made again as Paul lists the acts of the sinful nature in his letter to Christians in the province of Galatia and the city of Colosse. He writes:

> The acts of the sinful nature are obvious: sexual immorality, impurity and debauchery; idolatry and witchcraft; hatred, discord, jealousy, fits of rage, selfish ambition, dissensions, factions and envy; drunkenness, orgies, and the like.
>
> I warn you, as I did before, that those who live like this will not inherit the kingdom of God. (Galatians 5:19-21)

> But now you must rid yourselves of all such things as these: anger, rage, malice, slander, and filthy language from your lips. Do not lie to each other, since you have taken off your old self with its practices and have put on the new self, which is being renewed in knowledge in the image of its Creator. (Colossians 3:8-10)

The ugliness and evil associated with bad anger is clearly described by the New Testament writer James:

> *My dear brothers, take note of this: Everyone should be quick to listen, slow to speak and slow to become angry, for man's anger does not bring about the righteous life that God desires. (James 1:19-20)*

There is no way to walk high on the mountain of spirituality while being mired in the pit of anger. *"Man's anger does not bring about the righteous life that God desires."* To live in anger is to die to God. Anger causes a person to be spiritually depleted and defeated. It will stifle prayer life. It will destroy joy. It will take away hunger for the Word of God. Unresolved anger is a serious spiritual problem!

Mark it down. Sin is always at the root of bad anger.

The Opposite Of The Sin Of Anger

In our efforts to understand the nature of sinful anger, let's approach the topic from the reverse side. What biblical word can you think of that pinpoints the opposite of sinful anger? What spirit lives in a person when his or her anger is under God's control? The answer is meekness. Meekness is a good biblical word that describes the spirit of a person who has learned to live under the control of God.

But, who wants to be "meek?" Even the word is a major turnoff to many. "Meek" rhymes with "weak" and most people in today's hard-hitting world have no desire to be described as a meek person. Jim Kane in *Gentleness—The Gracious Fruit* tells about the man who founded a support group called the "Dependent Order Of Really Meek And Timid Souls"—known by its initials as "DOORMATS." Their official insignia is a yellow caution light. Their motto is, "The meek shall inherit the earth, if that is okay with everybody."

The truth is that meekness is the opposite of weakness. "Meekness" is "strength and power under God's control." The two people in the Bible who are referred to as "meek" men are Moses and Jesus. Neither was weak or passive in standing up for God! Moses stood before Pharaoh and boldly said, *"Let my people go!"* (Exodus 5-11) Moses expressed the anger of God because of the oppression of his people, yet the anger was vented in a spirit of meekness. Jesus was a meek man, but He was never weak. He taught and led with a spirit of authority, courage, and strength from God, yet he could say about himself, *"I am gentle (meek) and humble in heart."* (Matthew 11:29)

Anger Control Exercise 1

1. Let's get specific as we think about the connection between sin and anger. As you consider the sinful anger being expressed by the people who are mentioned below, try to pinpoint one specific sin that was a "major driver" in the situation.

   a. In *Genesis 4:1-12,* the anger of Cain was being driven by the sin of _____.

   b. In *Numbers 20:1-13,* the angry action of Moses in striking the rock was fueled by the sin of _____. (For additional background material, read *Numbers 11:11-15.*)

   c. Read *2 Kings 5:1-14.* The sin of _____ was prompting the anger of Naaman.

   d. Based on what you read about the "older brother" of the Prodigal in *Luke 15:11-32,* what specific sin was at work in his heart?

   _____

   e. The sinful anger of the Ephesians in *Acts 19:23-34* was rooted in the sin of _____.

2. How does John describe sinful anger in *1 John 3:15?*

3. In our battle with sinful anger, against whom are we fighting according to *Ephesians 6:10-18?* Who is our chief enemy as we battle anger?

4. "Meekness" was identified as the opposite of sinful anger. How do you view "meekness"? Is it a quality you desire? Is meekness understood by our culture-at-large? If not, how can this be changed for the better?

5. Anger can be at the root of many sins. Can you identify other sins that may be rooted in anger? When you are angry in a sinful way, what other sins may be stirred and committed?

6. Carefully read and study *Philippians 2:2-8*. Then list the attitudes and principles within this passage that, if applied, would help you to avoid sinful anger and lingering bitterness.

Determining Origin And Cause Is Not Always Easy

Discovering and dealing with the real causes of our anger can be a painful and difficult task. Why? Because when we are in the grip of anger, there may be so much raw emotion stirring. There can be such deep pain. The wounds may be old. Someone in your past may have abused you. A friend owes you money. A marriage partner abandoned you. The job you wanted was given to someone else. The children you reared rejected your love and leadership. A trusted friend let you down. Owning these painful realities can be extremely difficult. The big picture is not always easy to see and embrace.

Practicing objectivity with ourselves and others can be very hard. When the fires of anger are raging, it can even be difficult to hear the Word of God. Instead of seeing and dealing directly with the realities behind our anger, many are willing to live in denial of it. The truth can be too difficult to sort out or too painful to endure. Dealing with anger-issues is rarely easy.

Anger Control Exercise 2

1. How would you describe your mental state when you are angry? How can anger affect your ability to perceive reality and make good decisions?
2. What is the message of *Proverbs 14:16-17 and 14:29?*

When Sinful Anger Toward Others Is Living Within You

Are you willing to confess the sin of anger to God *(1 John 1:9)* and to those you have hurt? *(Luke 15:18-20)* It is never easy or pleasant to admit our own moral failures. No one enjoys saying, "I have committed the sin of anger due to my own insecurity, immaturity, or selfishness." How humiliating to have to admit to God, to myself, and to others that I have acted foolishly and expressed my anger in a sinful way.

Once we, in penitence, confess the sin of anger, then we must seek and rely upon the help of the Holy Spirit so that we don't return to a spirit of bitterness and rancor. Through His Word, God will help us. Through His Spirit, God will give us inward strength to walk in love rather than anger.

> *So I say, live by the Spirit, and you will not gratify the desires of the sinful nature.*
>
> *The acts of the sinful nature are obvious:* [Note how many of these are easily associated with sinful anger.] *sexual immorality, impurity and debauchery; idolatry and witchcraft; hatred, discord, jealousy, fits of rage, selfish ambition, dissensions, factions and envy; drunkenness, orgies, and the like. I warn you, as I did before, that those who live like this will not inherit the kingdom of God.*
>
> *But the fruit of the Spirit is love, joy, peace, patience, kindness, goodness, faithfulness, gentleness and self-control.* [Note how many of these are the solution to sinful anger.]

Since we live by the Spirit, let us keep in step with the Spirit. (Galatians 5:16, 19-23, 25)

For this reason, I kneel before the Father, from whom his whole family in heaven and on earth derives its name. I pray that out of his glorious riches he may strengthen you with power through his Spirit in your inner being, so that Christ may dwell in your hearts through faith. And I pray that you, being rooted and established in love, may have power together with all the saints to grasp how wide and long and high and deep is the love of Christ, and to know this love that surpasses knowledge—that you may be filled to the measure of all the fullness of God.

Now to him who is able to do immeasurably more than all we ask or imagine, according to his power that is at work within us, to him be glory in the church and in Christ Jesus throughout all generations, for ever and ever. Amen. (Ephesians 3:14-21)

Anger Control Exercise 3

1. If a person is hypersensitive and has a tendency to get angry easily, often, and without justification, what possible underlying personal struggles and vulnerabilities could be contributing to this problem?

2. Read *Luke 15:11-32.* The older son became angry when his younger brother left his life of sin and returned home. Analyze the anger of this older brother. Had he been willing to confess the sinfulness of his anger, how would his confession have been worded?

3. What is the message of *Ephesians 3:16-20?* What is the practical message for us as we fight the fires of sinful anger?

When The Sinful Anger Of Others Is Vented Toward You

There are times when we are on the receiving end of sinful anger. This can be devastating to the human spirit. Have you been there? It can be extremely painful and damaging to stand in the line of fire as someone vents sinful anger in your direction. For the angry offender to glibly say to you, "Just get over it," is not an adequate response. Neither is it helpful for some pious observer to offer the platitude, "Just turn it over to the Lord." Such responses reflect a failure to understand the "cause and effect" factor.

When you are feeling deeply hurt and angry because you have been treated unjustly, then the people and issues related to those feelings of hurt, betrayal, and abuse must be properly confronted as a part of the healing process. When possible, it is best to deal openly and honestly with the offender. To attempt to "swallow your anger" without dealing with the people and causes behind it can be little more than a painful exercise in "swallowing fire." *(Matthew 18:15-17)*

When anger issues are not addressed in a healthy and honest manner, the fires of anger may move underground and silently smolder. Even though the fire is not seen, it continues to seethe. And, smoldering embers can quickly burst into flames with sinful anger being vented in inappropriate ways, at inappropriate times, and at inappropriate objects.

Anger Control Exercise 4

1. Why is it difficult to "get over anger" when the problem behind the anger is never addressed or resolved?

2. Read *Matthew 5:23-24; 18:15-17*. How do the principles in these verses relate to the idea that it is important to deal directly with the people and issues related to your lingering feelings of anger?

Facing Our Offenders Is Not Easy

In some cases, we are reluctant to deal with the causes of our anger because we fear the negative reactions that might occur on the part of others who would need to be confronted. Facing offenders can be scary to you and offensive to them. Often times we opt to bury the offense within ourselves rather than to bare it to the one who may have hurt us. With this approach, we leave an emotional splinter buried within our spirit that can lead to chronic irritation, lingering resentment, or even hatred.

Anger Control Exercise 5

1. Why can fear be such a powerful factor in keeping offended persons from facing their offenders? What are the risks that cause people to decide that it is safer to stay angry than to confront an offender?

When Your Anger Is Directed Toward God

This can be hard to admit, but it's true. We find ourselves in situations where we are angry with God, feeling that He has let us down in some significant way. Such anger usually arises in times of great suffering and loss. Disease threatens to shatter your dreams. Death takes a precious loved one from your family. Desertion and divorce shake the foundations of your world. In such times, individuals can become very angry with God.

Clearly this is not a new phenomenon. You see this in many places in the Bible. For example, the Psalms contain many passages where hurting humans are crying out to God in their frustration and pain.

> But I cry to you for help, O Lord; in the morning my prayer comes before you. Why, O Lord, do you reject me and hide your face from me? (Psalm 88:1-14)

Even Jesus cried out from the cross, *"My God, my God, why have you for-saken me?" (Matthew 27:46)* In these difficult times, it is good to vent your honest feelings. God is our Father. He wants His hurting children to cry out to Him. You are likely to find that as you express your deep feelings, it is easier to be submissive to God and to deal in a productive way with the painful realities that may be affecting your life.

Anger Control Exercise 6

1. Read *Ruth 1*. What do you see in the spirit and life of Naomi that reflects anger toward God because of her circumstances?
2. Read *Jonah 3:10-4:1*. With whom was Jonah angry and why?
3. Have you ever experienced anger toward God because of the trials and tribulations in your life? Has this anger been properly resolved? If not, will you share it with a trusted friend and pray about the matter?

When Contact With The Offender Is Not Possible

In some cases, there are barriers—death, divorce, unknown locations and identities, and the like—that make it impossible for us to communicate with the people who have hurt us. This blocks the path to resolution. For example, where lines of communication no longer exist between the offender and the offended, it is impossible for words of love, confession, and forgiveness to be spoken. In such cases, we must find a way to help the angry person immerse the fires of his or her anger in the deep sea of God's love and grace. Holding on to bitterness and anger is so toxic. With God's help, we must begin the process of letting go.

Anger Control Exercise 7

1. What principles do you see in *Colossians 3:12-14* that could help the individual who cannot communicate directly with those who may be at the root of his or her anger?

We May Need Help To Know The Specific Cause Of Anger

In some cases, it is possible for a person to be clueless as to the origin of his or her chronic anger. Some have a bad day every day. They have a chip on both shoulders. A person might sincerely say, "I know I am angry, but I don't know why I am angry." Obviously, this condition of mind complicates and delays the process of anger resolution.

When the root of your anger is so hidden that you cannot clearly identify it, the assistance of others can help—trusted friends or qualified counselors. In many cases, a loving church family provides a safe and secure environment in which we can find suitable channels to assess, confess, and address our anger issues. In cases where an anger problem may be rooted in physiological infirmities, chemical imbalances, or psychological deficiencies, other specially qualified caregivers will need to be consulted.

In this search for the causes of anger, we must be careful not to needlessly stir the fires that may have already caused major damage in lives and relationships. We must use prayer and wisdom as we deal with sensitive issues and seek to heal existing wounds. The goal must always be restitution, resolution, and reconciliation. The objective is not to stoke the existing fires of sinful anger, but to put them out—for good.

Anger Control Exercise 8

1. Read *Philippians 4:2-3*. What was required in this situation to bring about a resolution between two sisters in Philippi who had differences? What is the practical implication for us?

2. God wants us to live in peace with each other. In this connection, what important principle is taught in *Romans 12:18?*

The Heart Of Our Anger Problem Is...The Heart

As painful as it may be to admit, the truth is that the fires of sinful anger always point to a "HEART PROBLEM." The God of peace—the God who is love—cannot continue to live in a heart that is filled with lingering bitterness, anger, or hatred.

Helpful Insights From This Chapter To Remember And Use...

1.

2.

3.

4.

Chapter 6

The Types of Anger—Yours?

There Are Different Types of Fire

In Firefighting 101, student fire fighters learn that there are different types of fire—Class A, B, C, and D. Class A fires are approached and extinguished in a way different to Class B, C, and D fires. For example, a Class A fire is fueled by things like wood, paper, and rubbish. On the other hand, a Class B fire involves flammable chemicals and liquids. Both classes can be potentially dangerous fires, yet their characteristics are different and they must be dealt with in different ways. In an emergency situation, one of the first things firefighters must do is identify the particular type of fire they are dealing with and fight it accordingly.

Understanding The Different Types Of Anger

Just like there are different types of physical fire, there are also different types of anger. Yes, based on your temperament, personality, childhood environment, and the depth of your walk with Christ, you do have an "anger-type" that is fairly predictable. Are you aware? Have you figured this out? We are people of habit and patterns of behavior can be identified as we practice careful observation and personal honesty. Knowing your "anger-type" is an important factor in the battle to control anger. This calls for further explanation. Consider the following story.

Illustrating Various Types Of Anger

Imagine two people in the same city on the same day each purchasing an identical sports car—except for color—from the same dealership. One chooses a red car, the other a beautiful green one. After closing the deal, both buyers exit the dealership parking lot thrilled with their new wheels. One goes east and the other turns west. Five minutes later, both cars are rear-ended by drunk drivers—total losses. It's reaction time! Suddenly, both drivers are burning with frustration and anger. But, how do they process and express their anger in these post-collision moments? Can we identify the "anger-types" of these two drivers?

The driver of the red car explodes at the accident scene with looks, words, sounds, and gestures of intense anger. There is a major eruption! At the sight and sound of crushed metal and shattered glass, an emotional explosion occurs! Boom! This driver emerges from the wrecked vehicle with anger oozing from every pore in his body. It's obvious to everybody at the accident scene that he is on fire with anger! With strong words, sharp tones, painful groans, irate accusations, and body gestures that demonstrate his feelings of rage, the driver of the red car is openly venting his fury! His anger is easy to see—and hear!

On the other hand, the reaction of the driver of the green car is very different—at least on the surface. Is she frustrated? Yes! Deeply so. Is she angry over what has occurred to her new vehicle? Yes—in fact, she is just as angry as the driver of the red car. But, the visible reactions are noticeably different. With this driver, there is no sudden flash of anger. No loud accusations are heard by witnesses at the scene. No visible displays of outrage. Instead, when the collision occurs, this driver buries her head in her hands and anguishes quietly in disbelief. She does not even exit the car.

In deep emotional pain, she begins to tremble. Sweat is pouring from her body. She suddenly experiences unbearable anxiety. A feeling of panic sets in. She is nauseous. Distraught. Life has dealt her another painful blow—another major disappointment. Deep inside herself, she ponders questions like, "Why did this happen to me? What have I done to deserve this? Where is God?" Emotionally, she sinks into a dark well of depression that will significantly affect her ability to function for days to come.

The external circumstances surrounding the two accidents are very similar. Property losses…the same. Feelings of disappointment…the same. Frustration and anger levels…the same. Yet, two very different ways of processing and expressing anger. What about "anger-types?"

"Pressure Cooker" Vs "Crock-Pot" Anger

Various writers have used pressure cookers and crock-pots to illustrate "anger-types." When a pressure cooker is too pumped with pressure, the lid comes off! This illustrates what occurs when people explode with anger. Others display an anger that resembles what happens in a crock-pot— stewing and steaming over an extended period of time. The man in the red car was the over-pressurized cooker. The woman in the green car was the crock-pot.

Some Are "Revealers" And Others Are "Concealers"

Anger has different faces. It surfaces in many different ways. The pattern for some is to consistently "reveal" their anger. Their tendency is to blow and spew. Others tend to "conceal" anger—at least for a time. They brood and stuff. Some throw anger up on everybody else. Others swallow their anger and attempt to process it internally. What type anger do you most often exhibit?

Obviously, the driver of the red sports car was a "revealer." He revealed his anger in an unhealthy and sinful way! He blew and spewed the heat of his anger on everyone at the accident scene. The lid came off!

In contrast, the driver of the green car responded as a "concealer" of anger. The fire of her wrath turned inward and took its toll on her body, mind, and spirit. She practiced an unhealthy and dysfunctional conceal-ment. She kept the lid on, but the internal pressure was very intense and damaging. Anger is difficult to conceal for very long.

Anger-Type #1...The Unhealthy And Sinful "Revealer"

"Anger" is just one letter away from "danger." *(Proverbs 14:17)* "Blowers" can, literally, blow people away! As human blowtorches, they can blister and burn others around them—often those who should be dearest to them. They may curse God or yell at people. Filthy words pour out of their mouths. They swear. They degrade and demean the objects of their rage. They hurl and break things. Some opt to slam doors or put their fists through walls. They blame and shame. They threaten and make demands. The desire for vengeance can be powerful. There can be partially controlled violence or blind rage. Christian attitudes and actions—totally missing.

Common sense and self-control can be lost so quickly. As the heat of anger intensifies, there can be a form of spiritual and emotional insanity that sets in. We loose it! In its wake, sinful anger can result in destroyed relationships, wrecked friendships, split families, employment termination, physical injury, or even loss of life. This anger-type is always ugly and hurtful. Severe emotional burns are inflicted upon others within seconds. The fires of sinful anger are volatile and vicious.

Anger-Type #2...The Unhealthy And Sinful "Concealer"

Anger can get buried alive. On the surface, everything looks cool. But, on the inside, there is heat and the temperature may be rising rapidly. When anger issues are not addressed in an open and healthy manner, the fires of our indignation may move underground and silently smolder. Resentments get stockpiled. Even though the fires of anger are not visible on the surface, they continue to seethe and cause internal damage.

Some "concealers" deny their anger altogether. "Nothing's wrong," they say. These people shove their anger into the cellar of their lives and say, "I never get angry." Bruce Carter uses a great analogy when he says, "Burying our anger is like burying canisters of toxic waste. You can put the stuff underground and everybody thinks the problem is gone until months or even years later. People begin to have serious health problems because toxic waste has leaked out of the canisters. Denied anger is like that—it always manages to leak out in some way." In reality, it is very difficult, if not impossible, to truly conceal anger for very long.

Severe mood swings and depression are probably the most common signs of hidden anger. Depression is serious because it damages us physically, psychologically, spiritually, and relationally. *(Luke 15:25-32)* Feeling wounded, offended, and troubled, repressed anger can be deadly to the human spirit. There can be social withdrawal, an unwillingness to communicate or cooperate, and self-pity—pouting or emotional obstructionism. We put up those "chilly walls" between others and ourselves. Suppressed anger can come out in the form of sarcasm, complaining, nagging, or teasing. It can result in a spouse demanding or refusing sexual intercourse, flirtation, or involvement in an extramarital affair. Sleeping and eating patterns can be affected when anger is inappropriately harbored. And, who can concentrate or remain focused while in the grip of anger? Psychosomatic medicine links bitterness, anger, and hatred to all sorts of physical diseases. Some work hard to conceal it, but the hard fact is that harboring anger is very self-destructive.

Anger-Type #3…My Anger-Type Is "Mixed"—In Some Situations "I Reveal" And In Others "I Conceal."

Some of us "reveal" our anger in some situations and "conceal" it in others. We do both depending on whom we are with and where we are. Some are "concealers" in most instances, but occasionally flare up. Others usually respond as "revealers," but with certain people in special settings, they can show great restraint. We can be quite selective when it comes to the manner in which we process and deal with our anger. Standing in the kitchen, a person can be in a heated fit of rage, yet answer the phone with a calm and kind tone of voice. "H-e-l-l-o!" "Revealing anger" one moment, yet "concealing it" the next.

Anger-Type #4…Healthy Internal Restraint That Precedes Healthy External Expression

James writes, *"Everyone should be quick to listen, slow to speak, and slow to become angry."* (James 1:19) Slowness in getting angry is commended and commanded in the Scriptures. In most cases when anger-causing incidents arise, it is wise to proceed cautiously and prayerfully to allow time for proper assessment of what may be causing the anger and the best way to resolve it as quickly as possible. In such cases, what we are calling "concealment" is actually a healthy form of anger-control.

Delaying action allows the freedom to consider the consequences of all available options, and the time to pray and counsel with others. It is important to consider all points of view and decide when and if to confront. Proper thought and preparation can help us to respond with the mercy and grace of one who has been graciously forgiven by God.

> *A wise man fears the Lord and shuns evil, but a fool is hotheaded and reckless. A quick-tempered man does foolish things, and a crafty man is hated. (Proverbs 14:16-17)*
>
> *A patient man has great understanding, but a quick-tempered man displays folly. (Proverbs 14:29)*
>
> *A gentle answer turns away wrath, but a harsh word stirs up anger.*
>
> *A hot-tempered man stirs up dissension, but a patient man calms a quarrel. (Proverbs 15:1; 18)*
>
> *A fool gives full vent to his anger, but a wise man keeps himself under control. (Proverbs 29:11)*

A delay in the venting of anger is to be temporary. At the proper time, with the right people, and in the appropriate way, anger must be adequately expressed. Releasing anger can be a very constructive act. Anger is like an emotional splinter—you must get it out in order to heal. The Bible teaches attitudes and actions that open the way for anger to be properly expressed and vented. The key words for Christians are, *"In your anger, do not sin…"* (Ephesians 4:26) There is a way to be "good" and "angry" at the same time. In fact, expressing your angry feelings without hurting yourself or others is the healthiest way to be angry.

A Questionnaire To Confirm Your "Anger-Type"

Have you determined your "anger-type?" The questions that follow will help to confirm or contradict any conclusion that you have reached. The questions are for your own self-awareness and no measurement scale is provided for rating your answers. At the end, you will be the judge of what your responses mean. A "right answer" is a "truthful answer." If you wish to double-check your answers for accuracy, you may want to allow a person who knows you well to review them. (Make sure "this review" can be carried out without setting off an anger explosion.) At the end of the questionnaire, hopefully you will be in a better position to accurately assess or confirm your anger-type.

1. ____ Yes ____ No   I am "a revealer" of my anger. In most cases, I do not stuff anger down inside of me.

2. ____ Yes ____ No   The people who know me best see me as one who tends to be calm and cool under pressure. When angry situations arise in my life, my pattern is to control my temper and seek to resolve the problem in a peaceful and helpful manner.

3. ____ Yes ____ No   My anger-type is mixed. In some settings, I blow and reveal my anger openly, whereas in other settings, I work hard to conceal my anger.

4. ____ Yes ____ No   If a drunk driver rear ended my new sports car on the day of purchase, I strongly suspect that I would demonstrate signs of rage at the accident scene.

5. ____ Yes ____ No   When I am aggravated and irritated, I never curse or say things with a harsh and cutting tone. I can be very angry, and at the same time speak directly and honestly about the problem without raising my voice or projecting my feelings with a tone of voice that says, "Why do I have to put up with you?"

6. ____ Yes ____ No   If my marriage partner does or says something that hurts and offends me, I am quick to say, "You hurt and offended me by your words or actions." I do not remain quiet or show other signs of withdrawal due to anger toward my mate.

7. ____ Yes ____ No   With those closest to me, I tend to be a revealer. With others, I manage to do a better job of controlling and concealing my anger.

8. ____ Yes ____ No   In most cases, when I am angry, I do not sin against God. Most of the time, I practice self-control in the way I express and deal with my anger. Based on my anger patterns, I believe that God is pleased with the way I handle my anger.

9. ____ Yes ____ No   Within my family setting, people know that when I am angry, I will blow up and vent my anger in visible and vocal ways for everyone to see and hear. With me the lid tends to come off.

10. ____ Yes ____ No   In the family setting, I am known as one who "gets over it quickly." I do not want the sun to go down while there is anger between family members. I am a peacemaker and always try to open lines of communication so that conflicts can be resolved quickly and as peacefully as possible.

11. ____ Yes ____ No   In the work setting, I seem to have the ability to mark and maintain my legitimate personal boundaries without causing others to be greatly offended. I am a communicator in the workplace and in an overall way enjoy harmonious relationships with co-workers.

12. ____ Yes ____ No   In the work setting, I tend to speak up when I am offended. I don't mind marking my boundaries and letting people know when they are trespassing. Confrontation with co-workers is not so uncommon with me.

13. _____ Yes _____ No   I never demonstrate a spirit of "road rage." In traffic, I tend to practice the golden rule. I actually find pleasure in favoring other drivers and showing Christian courtesy.

14. _____ Yes _____ No   When I am in traffic and another driver suddenly cuts in or pulls out in front of me, I definitely make an effort to let the offender know that I am not happy. I know how to use a car horn to send a clear message.

15. _____ Yes _____ No   If a fellow Christian offends me, I try to find an appropriate way to approach the person and talk peacefully and prayerfully about the offense. This method of resolving conflict has worked for me more than once.

16. _____ Yes _____ No   If I observe someone cutting in front of me in a line, my strong tendency is to speak up and let the offender know that such behavior is not fair or acceptable to me and others in line.

17. _____ Yes _____ No   Like everyone else, I do get angry. However, I tend not to be one who "boils over" to burn others with my anger. At the same time, I am not one who becomes quiet, sullen, and withdrawn when I am angry. I "get my anger out" as quickly as possible, while trying to vent it in a constructive manner.

18. _____ Yes _____ No   At a ballgame where "my team" is competing, I don't mind showing my displeasure when an official makes a bad call. I'm not one to sit back and quietly "take it."

19. _____ Yes _____ No   If a drunk driver rear ended my new sports car, I would be very angry and hurt; however, I would be in full control of my anger at

the accident site and would contribute to a helpful and peaceful follow-up to the accident.

20. ____ Yes ____ No   I have neighbors who view me as a revealer of anger—a blower.

21. ____ Yes ____ No   I have a short fuse and don't have much patience for what I perceive to be laziness, incompetence, carelessness, or willful disobedience. When I encounter these behaviors, I tend to react with anger that can appear to be heated and harsh.

22. ____ Yes ____ No   Thinking about my patterns of anger behavior, I am one of those people who nearly always vents. When anger feelings stir within me, you can predict that they are going to "come out" in some fashion. I admit that I am a "spewer"—not a "stuffer."

23. ____ Yes ____ No   When I am angry, I am likely to get quiet, show signs of withdrawal, pout, sulk, and stew internally.

24. ____ Yes ____ No   There are people who tiptoe around me, at times, for fear that I will blow my lid and throw a fit.

25. ____ Yes ____ No   I believe that I am in living in close compliance with the principles taught in *Ephesians 4:26: "In your anger, do not sin: Do not let the sun go down while you are still angry."*

Anger Control Exercise 1

1. Assess your "anger-type" based on the responses you have made to the preceding questions. Which of the "anger-types" listed below best describes you?

_____ My strong tendency is to "reveal" anger in unhealthy and sinful ways.

_____ My consistent pattern is to "conceal" anger in unhealthy and sinful ways.

_____ My anger-pattern is varied. In some circumstances, I tend to "reveal" my anger with unhealthy and sinful behaviors. Yet, on other occasions, I find myself trying to "conceal" my anger in unhealthy and sinful ways. My anger-type seems to be mixed.

_____ In an overall sense, I believe that I am showing progress in handling my anger by exercising "proper control" and then "expressing my anger in healthy and non-sinful ways."

Anger Control Exercise 2

1. In each of the Scriptures listed below, anger is being displayed by someone. Your assignment is to pinpoint the "anger-type" in each case. On the line beside each passage, put the letter from the list below (A, B, or C) that best describes the "anger-type" being displayed in each passage.

A. An unhealthy and sinful "revealing" of anger.

B. An unhealthy and sinful "concealing" of anger.

C. A healthy control and expression of anger that is not sinful.

_____ Saul's anger in *1 Samuel 20:30-34*

_____ Jonathan's anger in *1 Samuel 20:30-34*

_____ David's anger in *2 Samuel 12:1-10*

_____ The man described in *Proverbs 16:32*

_____ The man described in *Proverbs 29:22*

_____ King Herod in *Matthew 2:16*

_____ The worshipper in *Matthew 5:23-24*

_____ Peter *(John 18:10)* in *Matthew 26:51-54*

_____ James and John in *Luke 9:51-56*

_____ The older brother in *Luke 15:25-32*

2. Read *Psalm 139:1-6*. What do we need to remember when we are expending large amounts of energy to sinfully conceal our anger?

Helpful Insights From This Chapter To Remember And Use...

1.

2.

3.

4.

Chapter 7

The Effects of Anger—Where?

Fire Can Result in Great Loss

One moment you have the typical stuff that makes life…life—a house or apartment, clothing, furniture, household goods, appliances, pets, and whatever else. Suddenly, fire breaks out and within minutes you have practically nothing but the clothes on your back.

You walk through the ashes and rubble looking for items to salvage. There is sadness, disbelief, and a sickening sense of loss. Maybe it wasn't a mansion, but it was your home and your belongings—all the things you had worked hard to provide. Gone! And, the items that mattered the most are irreplaceable. Multiply the trauma of it all, many times over, if precious lives were lost.

Many of the losses of a house fire are evident the day it occurs—the loss of life, or health, or property and possessions. But recovery can be an unfolding of more and more loss. The disruptions continue, and the effort to piece lives back together can be stressful and heartbreaking at times.

Fire Can Cause First…Second…Or Third Degree Burns

When fires break out, people can get burned and suffer great losses. The severity of a burn depends upon its size, depth, and location. Medically, burns are classified by the degree of their severity.

FIRST DEGREE burns are the least severe. They are characterized by redness or discoloration, mild swelling, and pain.

SECOND DEGREE burns are more serious. They are deeper than first degree burns, look red or mottled and have blisters. They may also involve loss of fluids through the damaged skin. Second degree burns are very painful because nerve endings are usually intact, despite severe tissue damage.

THIRD DEGREE burns are the deepest. They may look white or charred, extend through all skin layers. Victims of third degree burns may have severe pain—or no pain at all if the nerve endings are destroyed.

Anger Can Have Serious Effects

Anger is like fire. It inflicts painful burns on others. It damages and destroys. Though we have no scientific way to measure the severity of the damage, the fact is that sinful anger can inflict first, second, or third degree emotional burns on others. Words can burn like hot flames. Looks can blister like hot coals. Physical violence can ravage like a raging wildfire. Even silent rejection and passive-aggressive anger can result in deep hurt and long-term scars. Anger must be treated with great caution in view of its potential effects. The evil effects of anger are innumerable.

Sinful Anger Affects Your Body

In some cases, you can actually see effects of anger on the physical body. Have you looked in a mirror when you are mad? Try it. Anger shows. It can make an attractive person look unattractive. The scowl on the face, the fire in the eyes, the coloring in the complexion, the trembling in the body, the pitch and tone of the voice, the gestures and body language—yes, anger can have powerful external effects on our bodies.

Anger also causes damage to our bodies internally. Anger that seethes and stays—chronic anger—can be extremely dangerous to one's health. Buried anger can be a cancer that quietly destroys or a ticking time bomb just waiting to explode. In either case, it will cause damage! What you don't see will hurt you. Anger causes physiological and biological changes within the body—blood pressure and body chemistry are altered in the wrong direction. Adrenaline is pumping—which is acceptable for the short-term, but very damaging if it continues long-term. Loss of sleep may occur. Eating patterns may change. Medical science has proven that anger can be at the root of headaches, stomach problems, heart and artery disease, and other physical ailments.

Anger can be "enjoyable" in a sick kind of way. You can lick your wounds, nurse your hurt feelings, and wait for a chance to retaliate. You can feast on your anger for a time. But, beware. The long-term problem is that what you are wolfing down is yourself! The skeleton at the feast is…you.

Anger Control Exercise I

1. In *Genesis 4:1-8*, the anger of Cain toward his brother is described. How did anger affect him physically?
2. Do you think strong feelings of anger affect your countenance as in the case of Cain? Do others know when you are angry by your outward appearance? How does anger "show" externally in your body?
3. How do you think strong feelings of anger tend to affect your body internally? Briefly describe that awful feeling that comes over you when you are mad. How does anger affect your appetite, social life, home life, performance at work, and overall outlook on life?

Sinful Anger Is Destabilizing To The Mind

Anger messes with your mind—it distorts reality and takes away good judgment. It makes concentration extremely difficult if not impossible. Lingering anger can suddenly release a mental fog that makes your world look dark and dismal. As the fog rolls in, you can feel that you are at the mercy of a powerful emotion that you cannot control. Anger can cause a person to lose his or her sense of proportion and display a form of mental insanity that leads to thoughts, words, and actions that you later regret. Anger can actually cause one to be so "hot-headed" that he or she acts irrationally and dangerously. Yes, anger affects the mind, which in turn affects behavior.

Complicating matters is the fact some angry people seek relief from their misery through other compulsive and dangerous behaviors such as smoking, drinking, drugs, illicit sex, workaholism, or perfectionism. Uncontrolled anger is a major cause of crime. Lingering anger will destabilize the mind, impair problem-solving abilities, and lower one's performance capabilities.

Anger Control Exercise 2

1. How is the quick-tempered man described in *Proverbs 14:17, 29?*
2. Comment on the wisdom behind the anger-related words in *Titus 1:7.*
3. In *Colossians 3:5-11,* Paul describes the evils of our earthly nature. What does he say is the power that can overcome the evil nature and transform us to be like our Creator?
4. Do the words of *Philippians 4:8* contain a practical and workable solution to sinful anger? Why are these words difficult to apply in times of anger?

Sinful Anger Is Destructive Spiritually

Sinful anger causes great damage to the inner person. It depletes and defeats us spiritually. Consider again the powerful words of Paul:

In your anger, do not sin. Do not let the sun go down while you are still angry, and do not give the devil a foothold. (Ephesians 4:26-27)

Armies that can establish a beachhead or a "foothold" have a distinct advantage over their enemies. A "foothold" is a base of operation. With a foothold, an army is able to dig in and wage war. What a horrible thought—Satan establishing a "base of operation" within my heart!

Have you played a game of tug-of-war? The key to winning this game is to establish a foothold. The team that is able to "dig in" has leverage and can exert a pull on the opponents that begins to pull and move them toward defeat. Once you have them moving in your direction, the goal is to increase the speed of the pull so that they are not able to establish a foothold. Satan gains leverage and weakens us spiritually when anger is not resolved quickly. Beware!

Anger Control Exercise 3

1. What anger-related warning do you see in *Hebrews 12:14-15?*

2. What anger-related truth is taught in *I John 3:14-15?*

3. What important truth is taught in *Romans 12:17-21* that will protect us from the poison of anger?

4. When anger dominates your spirit, how are spiritual disciplines affected—prayer, Bible study, meditation, ministry, church assemblies, evangelism and others?

Uncontrolled Anger Wreaks Havoc Within Our Society

We see it in road rage, in crime, in random violence, in terrorism, in the athletic arena—sadly it's even present in our divided churches. Uncontrolled anger burns the fabric of our society and leaves us feeling insecure and threatened. More and more, anger seems to be etched into people's lives. Could it be an indication of our physical fatigue, our spiritual bankruptcy, our emotional brokenness, and our lack of inner peace?

Anger Control Exercise 4

1. What is the important truth taught in *Proverbs 22:24-25?*
2. Do you feel that our society shows signs of being angrier than we were 50 years ago?
3. Is the stress and fear of living in an angry world causing us to be uptight and on edge? Are people consciously or unconsciously awaiting the next "9-11?" Does this tend to raise the level of anger? Explain.
4. In what ways should *"faith, hope, and love"* lower anger levels for Christian believers?

Sinful Anger Creates Problems In The Daily Workplace

Frustrations at work are natural and normal. How we deal with them determines how destructive they become. When these frustrations can be channeled in a positive direction, they can actually help an organization achieve.

Anger becomes destructive when it festers and turns into personal attacks, divisiveness, intimidation, harassment, unfairness, bullying, or even violence. Such conditions cause workers to feel like loners and outsiders. The workplace becomes an angry place. People are disgruntled most of the time. With the pressures of the workload, little down time, and the blending of many different temperaments and personalities, angry conflicts are bound to occur. An occasional flare-up is one thing, but a workplace that is seething is quite another.

Anger Control Exercise 5

1. How do you rate your job-related anger quotient?

    _____ I experience no anger due to circumstances related to my job.

_____ I experience only moderate levels of anger due to circumstances related to my job.

_____ I experience a high level of anger due to job-related experiences.

2. What conditions or relationships related to your daily work are creating serious anger issues and problems for you?

3. What is your plan for resolving these problems or effectively coping with these conditions or persons in the future?

Sinful Anger Is Damaging Within The Family Circle

Christian marriage mates get angry. But, they do not stay angry, and they learn to live with longer spaces between their angry moments. Chronic anger will choke and eventually smother a marriage relationship. The qualities that cause human relationships to grow and blossom cannot exist in an atmosphere of rancor and lingering bitterness. Anger eliminates mutual respect, blocks communication, prevents intimacy, and destroys friendship—love is starved to death.

Anger levels can rise to dangerous levels when generations clash on the home turf. Parents pull one way. Kids pull the other. Tug-of-war. Friction causes heat. Heat turns to anger. At best, sparks fly and the anger is resolved. Tragically, there are other situations where sparks lead to flames and precious people get blistered, burned, scarred, or even destroyed.

Anger Control Exercise 6

1. When it comes to the presence and resolution of anger, what should be different about family life for Christians as compared to others?

2. What important anger-related truth is taught in *Ephesians 6:4*?

3. Identify three key areas in the matter of building strong relationships that, if strengthened, would lower anger levels in many marriages today.
4. Of the three areas mentioned in the previous question, which one needs the most attention in your personal situation?

Fire-Related Headlines Tell The Story

The painful effects of fire are often highlighted in the headlines of newspapers the day after the tragedy occurs. For example, you might read:

First Degree Burns Suffered In Bus Wreck
Baby Killed In Burning Apartment
Small Children Suffocate In House Fire
Chemical Explosion Results In Third Degree Burns
Senior Citizens Trapped In Flames
Families Left Homeless
Beautiful Home Left Gutted
Valuable Property Destroyed
Hearts Broken By Fire Loss
Dreams Shattered By Explosion

When physical fire burns out of control, the effects are always bad. The same is true of anger.

Writing The Headlines Of Your Anger-Experience

As painful as it may be, we need to come to grips with the harmful effects of sinful anger. If you have been burned by the sinful anger of other people, you know the painful results. If you have inflicted anger burns on the people around you, then you may know the problems, the grief, the shame, and the guilt that follow.

If you had to write the newspaper headlines describing the effects of sinful anger in your life, how would they read? In your anger, what pain have you inflicted on others? Or, as the object of someone else's anger, what hurt have you received?

Anger Control Exercise 7

 Warning! This may be a painful exercise. (For some, it should be completed in a private setting. The goal is to help—not hurt.)

The purpose of the exercise is to deepen our sensitivities to the harmful effects of anger. We may have caused injury to others by our sinful anger. Or, we may have been injured by the anger that others have directed toward us.

Where we have caused injury, we need to demonstrate remorse, repentance, and provide restitution—if possible. Where we have received anger injuries from others, we need to experience the healing power of forgiveness and love from God. Use this exercise to make you aware of the people you have hurt by your anger. And, use it to identify people with whom and situations with which you may still have anger issues that need to be resolved by the power of God. Let this exercise remind you of the people that you need to pray for, love, reach out to, or forgive.

Here's how the exercise works.

Below, there is a sample list of imaginary headlines describing the effects that our anger can have on others. After reading the sample list, write your own "headlines" that describe the effects that your anger has had on others. Get personal.

Then, there is another sample list of imaginary headlines that describe the effects that the anger of other people can have on us. After reading this sample list, write your own "headlines" that describe how the sinful anger of others may have adversely affected you. Let this be an exercise that moves you toward "resolution"—not "revenge."

Again, this could be a painful exercise, but hopefully it will have a sobering and life-changing effect as we come to grips with the damaging effects of sinful anger—the ones we have caused as well as the ones we have endured.

SAMPLE HEADLINES THAT ILLUSTRATE THE EFFECTS THAT OUR ANGER CAN HAVE ON OTHERS:

**Children Verbally Abused By Me—
A Violent Father**

**Husband Demeaned And Cursed By Me—
An Outraged Wife**

**Wife Physically Assaulted By Me—
An Abusive Husband**

**Parents Disrespectfully Attacked By Me—
An Angry Child**

**Employee Unfairly Criticized By Me—
A Frustrated Employer**

**Church Fellowship Disrupted By Me—
A Fed -Up Member**

Add your own *"headlines"* revealing the effects that your sinful anger has had on others:

1.

2.

3.

SAMPLE HEADLINES THAT ILLUSTRATE THE EFFECTS THAT THE ANGER OF OTHERS CAN HAVE ON US:

**My Self-Confidence Destroyed
By Over-Correcting Parents**

**My Self-Esteemed Damaged
By Verbally Abusive Father**

**Parents Feel Grief Because Of
A Hostile And Rebellious Child**

**My Heart And Body Bruised
By Violent Husband**

**My Personal Security Weakened
By Violent Family Life**

**Painful Marriage Experience
Due To Long-Term Bitterness**

*Add your own **"headlines"** below revealing the harmful effects that the sinful anger of others has had on you:*

1.

2.

3.

Helpful Insights From This Chapter To Remember And Use...

1.

2.

3.

4.

Chapter 8

Healing Anger Burns—Forgive! (Part I)

Burns Can Be Devastating Injuries

Burns to the human body are extremely painful. Even the minor ones can result in major discomfort. First-degree burns are superficial injuries that involve only the outer layer of skin. Generally, they heal quickly on their own. Second-degree burns occur when the first layer of skin is burned through and the second layer, the dermal layer, is damaged. These wounds are more serious and require a longer healing time. Third-degree burns involve all the layers of the skin. They are referred to as full thickness burns. They are the most serious and most complicated to treat.

Burns can result in lifelong scarring, disfigurement, dysfunction, and death. Frequently, they are complex injuries. In addition to the burn injury itself, a number of other body parts and functions may be affected—muscle, bone, nerves, blood vessels, and other vital organs. A critical part of burn management is assessing the depth and extent of injury. Burn depth always has an impact on the way a burn is treated and the amount of healing time that will be required.

Anger Burns Are Serious And Painful

Let's think about anger burns. In many ways, they are similar to burns that occur with physical fire. Displays of sinful anger can inflict emotional burns that are quite varied as far as their depth and severity. All are painful. Many are very damaging and slow to heal—they can be quite complex. Some never heal.

Most of us know, firsthand, the damage that anger can do. In a fit of rage, we may have blistered and blasted others with our fiery looks, words, gestures, or actions. And, at the other end of this spectrum, many of us have been on the receiving end of sinful anger. We have suffered emotional burns due to the anger that others have spewed in our direction. Whether you have been on the giving or receiving end of sinful anger, you know that the consequences are not good. Never underestimate the damage that can be caused by the fires of anger. Could it be that we have been emotional arsonists and didn't know it?

When my heart was grieved and my spirit embittered, I was senseless and ignorant; I was a brute beast before you. (Psalm 73:21-22)

Do not let any unwholesome talk come out of your mouths, but only what is helpful for building others up according to their needs, that it may benefit those who listen. Get rid of all bitterness, rage and anger, brawling and slander, along with every form of malice. Be kind and compassionate to one another, forgiving each other, just as in Christ God forgave you. (Ephesians 4:29, 31-32)

Who is wise and understanding among you? Let him show it by his good life, by deeds done in the humility that comes from wisdom. But if you harbor bitter envy and selfish ambition in your hearts, do not boast about it or deny the truth.

Such "wisdom does not come down from heaven" but is earthly, unspiritual, of the devil. For where you have envy and selfish ambition, there you find disorder and every evil practice.

But the "wisdom that comes from heaven" is first of all pure; then peace-loving, considerate, submissive, full of mercy and good fruit, impartial and sincere. Peacemakers who sow in peace raise a harvest of righteousness. (James 3:13-18)

Anger Control Exercise I

1. Have you been burned emotionally by the sinful anger that other people have directed toward you? In that connection, please respond to the following statements:

    a. Presently, I am suffering the pain of anger burns due to the wrath that someone else has channeled in my direction.

    _____ Yes _____ No
    (If "No," move to #2.)

    b. I know and can identify the person/s who inflicted these emotional burns on me.

    _____ Yes _____ No

    c. I have fully healed from these anger burns and harbor no lingering bitterness and hold no grudges.

    _____ Yes _____ No _____ Not Sure
    (If your answer is "Yes," move to #2)

    d. As one who continues to feel wounded and injured from emotional anger burns, I truly desire healing from the Lord. I want to forgive the ones who have hurt me. I want to get well.

    _____ Yes _____ No _____ Not Sure

    e. On the lines below, list the name/s of the people who have hurt you by their expressions of sinful anger. These are people that you need to approach in a loving way in an effort to make peace and bring about healing. *(Matthew 18:15-17)*

    _____

    _____

2. While venting your own sinful anger, have you inflicted emotional anger burns on other people? In that connection, please respond to the following statements:

   a.   I confess that I have spewed sinful anger on other people. In my anger, I have not only sinned against God, but have inflicted emotional anger-burns that have caused deep pain and extensive damage to other people.

   _____ Yes _____ No

   b.   I can identify the people that I have hurt with expressions of sinful anger. I know who they are and what I have done to cause them pain.

   _____ Yes _____ No

   c.   I have done all that I can do to express my sorrow and remorse to those I have hurt with my anger. I have asked God and those I have offended to forgive me.

   _____ Yes _____ No

   (If your answer is "Yes," move to the next section.)

   d.   I am ready and willing to do all that I can to make things right with the people I have hurt with my sinful anger.

   _____ Yes _____ No

   e.   On the lines below, list the name/s of people that you need to approach in a loving way in an effort to make peace and heal wounds caused by your sinful anger. (Matthew 5:23-24; Romans 12:17-18)

   _____

   _____

Forgiveness—The Healing Balm That Works

Do you recognize the following words and remember who uttered them?

> *Forgive us our sins just as we have forgiven those who have sinned against us. (Matthew 6:12, NLT)*

Yes, these are words of Jesus taken right out of the Lord's Prayer. *(Matthew 6:9-15)* He taught us to pray, *"Father, forgive us…as we forgive them."* Obviously, Jesus recognized the healing power and therapeutic value of forgiveness. It is the sure and certain path to healing. God has a healing balm for anger burns that will have amazing results. That balm is…forgiveness.

Let's Be Sensitive As We Study Forgiveness

Caution!

When people are fuming and burning with anger, forgiveness can be a delicate matter to bring up and an even tougher topic to work through. To tritely and lightly say, "You just need to forgive the person/s who hurt you!" can sound, to the offended one, as if you are trivializing and minimizing the offense. When wounds are raw, emotions running high, and pain extremely bad, the idea of forgiving the offender can cause angry people to feel even angrier. In calling for forgiveness, we must not appear to be "popping off" as if forgiveness is easy and quick. It's not!

Forgiveness Can Seem Impractical And Impossible

The truth is that forgiveness can be tough work. Finding your way through anger to the place of forgiveness is no simple challenge for many of us. When someone has injured your body, wounded your spirit, broken your heart, and shattered your dreams, forgiveness does not come easy. Human emotions rise up within us to strongly resist the idea of forgiveness. Get real! Get practical! The natural response to human hurt is "an eye for an eye and a tooth for a tooth." When someone clobbers you, forgiveness can seem absurd—like a dumb thing to do. If I have been attacked, I should "go the distance" to collect what is owed. Retaliate! Even the score!

Forgiveness can even seem impossible. The steel shackles of resentment, bitterness, and hatred chain us to the offense and the offender. Extending mercy and offering forgiveness can seem like an impossible thing to do.

Forgiveness is especially hard in situations where severe abuse has occurred.

Anger Control Exercise 2

1. What serious warning is given in *Matthew 6:14-15?*
2. Does our human nature prompt us to be forgiving when we are wronged? Do we naturally know how to forgive? What does human nature prompt us to do? (*Romans 8:5-8; Galatians 5:19-21*)
3. Read *Luke 17:1-5.* Briefly state what Jesus teaches on the subject of forgiveness. What do you make of the apostles' response as described in *verse 5?*
4. Read *Matthew 5:1-12.* Identify the Beatitudes that are in some way related to a spirit of forgiveness. Explain.

We Have A Model For Radical Forgiveness

When we are feeling the pain of anger burns that have been inflicted upon us, it is not uncommon to wrestle with the question: "How could I possibly forgive my offender/s?" It's a valid question that cannot be lightly dismissed.

However, there is another question with which we must wrestle as followers of Jesus Christ. Before we ask, "How can I forgive my offender/s?" we should first answer the question, "How can God forgive my offenses?" Once you discover what is behind God's forgiveness of your offenses, only then will you have the Master's key to answering the question, "How can I forgive my offender/s?"

Think about it. Every sin that we commit is a huge debt that we owe God. What does that mean as far as the size of our debt to Him? There are times that we sin against God several times in one hour. Multiply that by the weeks, months, and years. What an enormous debt. A debt that we can never repay! *(Romans 3:9-20)*

The words of a familiar song help us to get the picture.

> He paid a debt he did not owe,
> I owed a debt I could not pay.
> I needed someone to wash my sins away.
> And now I sing a brand new song: "Amazing Grace."
> Christ Jesus paid the debt that I could never pay.
>
> He paid the debt at Calvary,
> He cleansed my soul and set me free,
> I'm glad that Jesus did all my sins erase;
> I now can sing a brand new song: "Amazing Grace."
> Christ Jesus paid the debt that I could never pay.

Amazing grace! This is the "Master's key" to unlocking the door to forgiveness. "Grace." What an amazing power. What a healing balm. And the model for practicing "grace" has been beautifully demonstrated in the forgiving love that God has shown to each of us in Christ! Grace is the spirit that prompts us to say to our offender/s, "Because of what God has done for me in Christ, I want to give you what you need—not what you deserve." Amazing grace!

A Passage That Must "Get You" If You Are To "Get It"

As we struggle to practice "amazing grace" and extend forgiveness to our offender/s, may God help us to be firmly gripped and deeply moved by the message of *Matthew 18:21-35*. It's not enough for us "to get this passage." No! This passage must "get us." What is the message? Hopefully, the guided study that follows will motivate us to practice the "amazing grace of God" as we deal with the hurts and wounds of our lives. Read the biblical text as you work through the commentary that follows.

Matthew 18:21

Make sure you understand the context of this conversation between the Lord and Peter. The words of *Matthew 18:15-20* provide the contextual backdrop of the verses we are about to study.

Peter understands that offenses need to be resolved and wrongs need to be confessed and forgiven. Yet, he wants to know where the "cutting off" point is. When is it proper to say, "Enough is enough! That's it! No more forgiveness!" Most rabbis held the view that after three offenses, forgiveness is not required. Three strikes and "you're out!" Peter wanted to be generous. He doubled the "three offenses" and added one. He said, *"Lord, how many times shall I forgive my brother when he sins against me? Up to seven times?"* Giving someone "7 strikes" before he is out seemed extremely generous to Peter.

Matthew 18:22

Can you imagine the shock that Peter felt when he heard Jesus' reply. Jesus said, *"No Peter. Not seven times. Forgive seventy times seven!"* You don't need a calculator to interpret the meaning of Jesus' words. The key is to reflect upon the loving and forgiving heart of God toward us! When Jesus said, *"Forgive seventy times seven,"* he was using "celestial math." He was calling for unlimited forgiveness. Stop keeping score! Quit tracking! Jesus teaches lavish forgiveness! He calls for a spirit of forgiveness that goes far beyond any reasonable human limits.

To illustrate this powerful principle of unlimited forgiveness, Jesus tells a story.

Matthew 18:23

The story is about a great Oriental king who decided to call in all debts. He demands that all accounts be settled. It's time to pay up! The king in this story represents God. We are the debtors.

Matthew 18:24

One particular man owes the king a huge debt that would amount to 50 years of wages. For the sake of illustration, we will say that he owes more than a million dollars. What would he do? There was no way he could pay off the debt. His situation is hopeless.

Matthew 18:25

Because the debtor could not pay his debt, the king ordered that his entire family be hocked in lieu of the debt. This is worse than bankruptcy! What can the debtor do?

Matthew 18:26

In great agony, the debtor cringes before the king. He begs and pleads for mercy. He asks for more time to pay his just debt. In reality, he would not be able to pay the debt if he had another lifetime! His debt to the king was so enormous that it could never be paid. What would he do?

Matthew 18:27

The king demonstrated "amazing grace" toward the hopeless debtor. He did not merely give the indebted servant additional time to pay. Neither did he discount the debt. He didn't say, "Okay, I will put the punishment on hold, but you still owe the debt!" No! The king showed mercy and completely cancelled the debt. He gave the debtor what he needed—not what he deserved! Amazing grace set this debtor free! Completely free!

Matthew 18:28

Can you believe what this forgiven man did after receiving such a magnificent gift from the king? How could he? After receiving amazing grace from the king to whom he owed more than a million dollars, he encountered a man who owed him $20. "Pay!" he said to the man. In fact, he grabbed the poor fellow by the throat and choked him. "Pay now!" he yelled. The man who owed him $20 begged for mercy. He needed amazing grace.

Matthew 18:29

The $20 debtor continued to plead for mercy. On his knees, he begged, *"Be patient with me and I will pay you back."* Sound familiar? The plea of the second beggar was identical to what the first debtor had said when he appeared before the king. This pitiful second beggar says, "Please, give me mercy! Give me more time!" What is the response?

Matthew 18:30-31

Can you believe this? This man who had been forgiven a debt of more than a million dollars flatly refused to forgive the man who owed him $20! How can this be? Not only would he not forgive the debt, he would not even extend the time for repayment.

Others witnessed this unbelievable confrontation. They, in turn, told the king of this man's unmerciful and hard-hearted attitudes and actions. Then what?

Matthew 18:32-34

The king who had been so merciful called the unforgiving man in and said, *"You wicked servant. I cancelled all your debt because you begged me to. Shouldn't you have had mercy on your fellow servant just as I had on you?"* There's the core principle within the parable! If you want forgiveness from

God, you must be willing to extend forgiveness to others. What a sad out-come to the story. The king reinstated the million-dollar debt because this man was unwilling to forgive. And, then comes the clincher!

Matthew 18:35

Jesus closes this teaching by saying, *"This is how my heavenly Father will treat each of you unless you forgive your brother from your heart."* If you have been forgiven by God, then you must forgive others who sin against you.

Do you see why we say, "It's not enough for us "to get this passage." The powerful message of this passage must "get us."

We Must Understand How Lavishly We Have Been Forgiven

We owe a sin-debt to God that we cannot pay! We are totally helpless and powerless. Our only hope is that God will give us what we need and not what we deserve. We need grace. We deserve punishment. In show-ing His mercy, God does not dispense His grace a thimble-full at a time and tell us to spread it around as far as it will go. No! Our loving and forgiving God takes us as sinful and rebellious children and drops us into the ocean of His grace. It truly is…amazing grace!

> In Jesus, we have redemption through his blood, the forgiveness of sins, in accordance with the riches of God's grace that he lavished on us with all wisdom and understanding. (Ephesians 1:7-8)

Showing a spirit of forgiveness is God-like. *(Ephesians 4:22-24)* It is the way of strength and beauty. Contrary to the old proverb, revenge is never sweet. In one sense, we need to forget the sin-debt from which the blood of Jesus has freed us. We must forget it in the sense that we do not contin-ue to carry the load of guilt. Yet, in another sense, we must never forget that huge debt of sin against us that was cancelled by a gracious God. Because God has so freely forgiven us, we must be good forgivers! We for-give in order to be forgiven. And, we forgive because we are forgiven! Forgiveness is the "spiritual water" that puts out the fires of anger.

Anger Control Exercise 3

1. What thoughts and feelings come to your mind when you read the words recorded in *Luke 23:34?*

2. In *Ephesians 4:32* and *Colossians 3:13*, Paul repeats the key principle that is to motivate a forgiving spirit within us. What is that principle?

3. In *Matthew 5:43-45*, what powerful principle does Jesus teach that, if applied, would help us deal with our enemies in a loving and forgiving manner?

4. According to the truths taught in *Galatians 5:22-23* and *Romans 5:5*, whose help must we have if we are to show a spirit of forgiveness?

5. Doing "the right thing" is not always "the easy thing." Read *Romans 12:14-21*. Make a list of "the right things" we should do even though they are not "easy things" for us to practice.

6. As a research project, seek out a resource person who can demonstrate for you the deaf sign for "forgiveness."

Helpful Insights From This Chapter To Remember And Use...

1.

2.

3.

4.

Chapter 9

Healing Anger Burns—Forgive! (Part 2)

"The Book Of Hurts"—Could You Add A Chapter?

If there were a book entitled *The Big Book Of Hurts,* every person could add a chapter—or two…or three. What would be the focus of your entry? What colorful accounts of human hurt could you describe? How many pages would your stories fill? Yes, we've all been hurt somehow, somewhere, by somebody along the pathway of life. Jesus told us the truth when He said, *"In this world, you will have trouble." (John 16:33)*

So, what do we do with the hurts of life? The sinful nature within us continually prompts us to nurse, curse, and rehearse our painful wounds, while growing more and more resentful and bitter. *(Romans 8:5-8; Galatians 5:19-21)* The natural response is to hold on to grudges, while letting go of mercy and forgiveness.

Avoiding Over-Sensitivity

Is it possible that we have been guilty of adding chapters to *The Big Book Of Hurts* too often and unnecessarily? Are we enlarging this book unnecessarily? Could it be that some of us have been far too sensitive to many of the frustrations and irritations that we have encountered? So quickly our feelings are hurt and we become "victims" when we ought to "let it go" and live as "victors." Do you have some chapters recorded in *The Big Book Of Hurts* that need to be ripped out and thrown away? Have we been reading and re-reading these old chapters for too long? Sometimes we just need to "get over it." In some cases, the problem is not what others have done to us. It is what we are doing to ourselves.

Face it! We live in an imperfect world—marked and marred by sin. Every person you live and associate with is an imperfect person. And, along with all the imperfect people with whom you rub shoulders daily, there is one additional imperfect human being on the scene. You! This is reality. This is the way it is and the way it is going to stay until the Lord comes. Accept it! We all mess up. We bump and bruise each other. We must avoid making world wars out of minor skirmishes. Move on! By accepting this reality, we can learn to ignore, pass over, and forget many things that, previously, have caused us to become burdened and embittered.

Anger Control Exercise I

1. Read *Philippians 1:12-18.* This passage describes trials and tribulations that were being faced by Paul who was a prisoner for Christ. What do you see in Paul's attitude and actions that would seem to indicate that he had no desire to write a chapter about his troubles and add it to *The Big Book Of Hurts*?

When The Hurt Is Real And Will Not Go Away

Sometimes we are deeply hurt and the clichés "Get over it" and "Move on" only serve to deepen our wounds rather than heal them. Offenses can be very serious and the pain does not go away. When there has been crime, lying, cheating, betrayal, abuse, slander, and such, it is not easy to just "move on" and "get over it."

Pretending that an offense did not happen or that it really didn't matter to us, when it did, is to live in unhealthy and dishonest denial. To ignore an infected wound is not biblical or practical. By honestly admitting and facing the injury, we can then intentionally choose to walk a path that leads toward eventual forgiveness and healing. To live in a sick denial of our hurt only blocks the way to a path of healing. Thus, when hurts are deep and wounds are real, we must make wise choices about our course of action.

We must choose to pursue the path of forgiveness even though that path can appear long and difficult. No one said forgiveness is easy!

Anger Control Exercise 2

1. Spend a few minutes reading in the Psalms. Find a psalm or a portion of a psalm that reveals a writer who was being honest and open about the deep hurts of his life—no pretending or denial. Identify the psalm that you select and be prepared to share it with others.

Toward An Understanding Of Forgiveness

Forgiveness can seem beyond our reach simply because we are not clear about what forgiveness is and what it is not. In an effort to clarify the nature and meaning of forgiveness, consider the following truths.

1. *FORGIVENESS IS NOT SAYING THAT WHAT YOUR OFFENDER DID IS ACCEPTABLE AND OKAY.*

Think about how God deals with us. Yes, He forgives, but in His forgiving action, He never endorses or approves of our sin. He never says, "It's okay." In fact, He hates sin in our lives, yet while hating our sin, He forgives the sinner.

The selfish and sinful deeds of others that have caused hurt and hardship in your life are destructive behaviors. They are not okay and never will be. They must be repented of and given up! To forgive a person does not mean that you must act as if everything is wonderful and send the message, "Hey, it's okay. Do it again."

Forgiveness means that you decide to drop charges against the person who hurt you and give up the desire for revenge. Yet, those wrongs that were done to you are still wrong. Forgiveness is a decision that gets your heart right before God even though it does not make the hurtful actions of your offender right.

Anger Control Exercise 3

1. In *Acts 7:54-60*, we read about Stephen being stoned by his enemies. What was his prayer for these people? In his prayer, how does he refer to their actions? How did the Lord respond when He witnessed this act of persecution toward Stephen? (Hint: Several passages in the New Testament indicate that Jesus now *"sits at the right hand of God"* in heaven—*Ephesians 1:20; Colossians 3:1; Hebrews 1:1-3*. However, in *Acts 7:54-60*, Jesus is in a "standing posture." What message could this imagery convey?)

2. *FORGIVENESS IS NOT IDENTICAL TO RECONCILIATION.*

Some might say, "I cannot forgive because I am not ready to be reconciled to the person who hurt me." This statement reflects a misunderstanding. Forgiveness can occur even if reconciliation does not.

Forgiveness takes only one person—the person who has been hurt. Even if the offender is impenitent, cold, and uncaring, the offended one can choose to forgive. Hanging on the cross, with His offenders still offending, Jesus prayed, *"Father, forgive them."*

Reconciliation requires the hard work of two people—the person who has been hurt and the offender. The word "reconciliation" means, "to restore the relationship." In order for this to occur, both the offended one and the offender must be fully engaged in the healing process. Reconciliation requires forgiveness on the part of the one who has been hurt and repentance on the part of the offender. The one who committed the injury must take responsibility for it and demonstrate godly sorrow.

When the offender repents and the offended one forgives, reconciliation can occur.

It should be pointed out that even when there is reconciliation between two people, there may still be a legitimate distance that is created in the relationship—there may never be the warmth and closeness there once was even though the two parties are reconciled. The two parties can be cordial without being close.

Anger Control Exercise 4

1. Read *Acts 15:36-41*. What do you see in these verses to illustrate the fact that there may need to be the creation of a "legitimate space" in some relationships after there has been controversy and confrontation—even though there is no lingering bitterness or hatred?

2. How could such a "space" serve a useful purpose in facilitating healing? (The information in *2 Timothy 4:11* may be helpful.)

3. I CAN DEMONSTRATE A SPIRIT OF FORGIVENESS EVEN WHEN I DON'T FEEL LIKE FORGIVING.

When someone has hurt you deeply, you don't exactly feel like rolling out the red carpet and hugging his or her neck. You may be envisioning other things that you would like to do to this person's neck. When someone pops off and flippantly says, "Oh, I find it extremely easy to forgive," you can nearly always know that the individual has not faced severe human hurt and trauma. Yes, the Lord did forgive those who crucified Him, but few of us have the strength of character or the depth of obedience He had. Let a drunk driver kill your child, and see how easy it is to forgive. When a marriage partner cheats and leaves you for another person, forgiveness is not a piece of cake. When so-called friends slander your name, forgiveness can take on an entirely different look.

In order to forgive, we nearly always have to do something we don't feel like doing. This is hard in our "feel-good" culture. Our goal must always be the will of God. It's not primarily a matter of my feelings, but His will. As Jesus sweated blood in Gethsemane, He prayed, *"Father, remove this cup!"* He didn't feel like going to the cross, but ultimately He submitted to the will of His Father. We must follow His example.

Anger Control Exercise 5

1. Read *Luke 15:11-32*. Analyze the "feelings" of the father and compare them to the "feelings" of the older brother.
2. Had the father been hurt, disappointed, and offended by the sinful actions of the prodigal son? What prompted the father to put out the "Welcome Home" sign to a son who had hurt him so badly?
3. Describe the scene when the sinful son began to confess his faults to his father. What attitude did his father reflect?

4. FORGIVENESS IS AN EXERCISE IN MERCY—NOT JUSTICE.

The principles and rules of fairness do not apply when you are practicing the spirit of forgiveness. In our sinful nature, we tend to cry out for justice, which says, "If you repent of the wrong, apologize with sincerity, and make proper restitution, then I will cheerfully forgive." We like for our offenders to "earn their grace."

To practice forgiveness God's way, we must keep going back, again and again, to the cross. There was nothing "fair" about the suffering of Jesus that brought about our forgiveness. If you have been forgiven by God, it is not because you "worked out a deal" with the Lord or "negotiated a fair contract." No! The truth is that He paid it all when we deserved nothing but punishment!

Anger Control Exercise 6

1. Read *Romans 5:6-8*. What three words in these verses describe "our condition" before God when Jesus died for us?
2. What is the practical lesson on forgiveness for us in these verses?
3. What is the powerful lesson on love and forgiveness in *Titus 3:3-7?*

5. FORGIVENESS AND HEALING FROM THE WOUNDS OF LIFE TAKE TIME AND EFFORT.

Don't think that in one big giant leap you will be able to bridge the emotional and relational gaps that exist between you and the one who offended you. Forgiveness is a process that should be viewed as a series of steps that are taken over a period of time. The amount of time required will vary depending on the personalities involved and the depth of the injuries. This can be a confusing process because on one day you may be saying, "I forgive," yet the next day, with your emotions dragging you down, you may be saying, "No, I do not forgive." In the recovery from severe emotional burns, a person may experience a wild roller-coaster ride full of ups and downs.

Forgiveness is a decision to "drop the charges." Yet, full emotional healing may take much longer. Start with forgiveness. Drop the charges. Then, allow God to do His healing work in the days or months that follow.

Anger Control Exercise 7

1. Do you agree that an offended person can forgive—drop the charges against the offender—

yet still need additional time for full and complete emotional healing to occur? Share your thoughts and feelings on this matter.

2. How could Satan use this truth to influence the situation?

6. *FORGIVENESS IS NOT FORGETTING THE OFFENSE THAT OCCURRED.*

You've heard the admonition. "You must forgive and forget—now!" Forget? This harsh and demanding approach to forgiveness has caused many to give up and quit trying. Forgiveness does not mean that we must wipe from our memories the complete record of the wrongs that were committed against us. Brian Joyce writes, "Forgiving does not mean a change in memory, but a change in heart."

Forgiving does mean that we choose not to remember in the sense of dwelling and focusing on the offense and the offender. We refuse to allow the past to dominate the present and ruin the future.

Corrie ten Boom tells how her captors violated her in a malicious way. For a time, she was extremely bitter. Finally, she made the decision to forgive. Yet, during the many nights that followed her decision to forgive, she admits that she would awaken and get angry all over again. She confessed her frustration and failure to a friend. This friend responded with wise counsel. She said, "Corrie, do you see that bell tower in the building next door? When we pull the rope, the bell rings out. But, what happens when we let go of the rope? Slowly, the sound of the bell fades away. Corrie, forgiveness is somewhat like that. When we forgive, we take our hands off the rope. But, don't be surprised if old angry thoughts keep coming back for a while. They are just ding-dongs of old bells slowing down and fading away. Don't dwell on them and they will gradually die away. The good part is that when you let go of the rope, the force is gone out of your anger."

Anger Control Exercise 8

1. Comment on the idea that, in one sense, it may be wise to remember a hurt that you have received and the person who inflicted it. While this "remembering" should never be used as a basis for continuing bitterness and anger, it could be beneficial and helpful in some ways. Give your comments on this idea. What are your thoughts and feelings on this "healthy kind of remembering?"

Forgiveness Is Not Easy But It's God's Way

Because forgiveness is God's way, it must be our way. Is it easy? No! Is it right? Yes! To live in bitterness imprisons you in your past. Bitterness begets more bitterness. To refuse to move in the direction of forgiveness is to put a "welcome mat" out to Satan and a "do not disturb" sign out to the Holy Spirit. We must decide to begin the journey of forgiveness.

The spirit of forgiveness creates new beginnings out of old failures. The revenge-approach says, "An eye for an eye." But if we opt for that approach, we will all be blind. Revenge and lingering bitterness compound the problems and add to the human misery.

Frequently, true forgiveness can only be achieved by the supernatural power of God. Trusting God for strength, relying on His Word for guidance, depending on the Holy Spirit for help, and seeking the support of our fellow-believers, we can flush our hearts of sinful bitterness and experience the peace that can only come through "amazing grace."

Anger Control Exercise 9

1. Read each of the passages listed below, and then briefly describe the amazing "new beginnings" that occurred when "amazing grace" was shown to sinners.

    a. *Genesis 45:1-15*

b. *John 4:1-42*

    c. *John 8:1-11*

    d. *1 Corinthians 6:9-11*

Helpful Insights From This Chapter To Remember And Use...

1.

2.

3.

4.

Chapter 10

Anger Control—A Plan to Succeed!

The Need For a Plan of Escape

Do you remember fire drills? Hopefully, they are still occurring in our homes and workplaces. A loud warning is sounded and everyone responds immediately as if there were a major fire taking place. Knowing what to do in the midst of a crisis and following through are the keys to surviving most fire emergencies. A fire drill is nothing less than a well-thought-out plan to prevent injury and loss in the event of fire.

There are two steps for a good evacuation program—planning and practice. Planning gives you the information you need ahead of time to evacuate safely. Practice reduces panic and makes the escape much easier to execute should the moment of crisis come.

Do You Have A Plan To Control Your Anger?

Ever heard of an "anger drill"? Why not? The damaging fires of sinful anger threaten us frequently. Too often we live as if we are helpless victims of these fires. People say, "Oh well, I guess I'm just wired that way. I can't help my anger." No, as God's people, we can and we must learn to deal successfully with our anger. Preparation is essential. We need a plan. And, we need to put that plan into action.

Through Jesus Christ, we no longer have to be victimized by sinful anger. We can be victors over this powerful and deadly force. The key is to pray fervently, probe deeply, and plan adequately so that when the temptation to be controlled by sinful anger flares up in our faces, we will be spiritually equipped and emotionally prepared to remain in control of this powerful force. We must not be caught by surprise with our guard down.

With no plan to overcome the sin of anger, we make it easy for the adversary to overcome us. A failure to plan is a plan to fail. With no strategy to control sinful anger, we are easily controlled by the one who does have a strategy. *(2 Corinthians 2:11; Ephesians 6:11)* Because we are ill prepared, we keep making the same mistakes over and over again and allow Satan to have a foothold in our lives.

No more!

Can we not see the need for a prayed-out and planned-out strategy for controlling our anger? This applies to every person, but especially for those whose behavior patterns demonstrate a major weakness in this area. Recall the truth that it is always better to prepare and prevent than to repair and repent.

Working On A Plan To Successfully Control Anger

It's time!

Let's learn some good "mad skills" and put them into practice. It is time to formulate a new plan for succeeding and eliminate the old patterns of failing. Enough damage has been done. Enough pain has been endured. Enough scars have been inflicted. It is time for us to utilize the anger-controlling power and principles that God makes available to His children.

In this final chapter, let's work on an "anger-control drill" that will enable us to be successful anger-fighters rather than defeated anger-failures. In the pages that follow, you will be considering principles and practices from the Bible that, if applied, will enable you to be successful in controlling your anger. As each principle is singled out, you will be challenged to "personalize" the plan by actually writing down your own plan of action for overcoming sinful anger. It's time for action. It's time to make a commitment. It's time for change. One psychologist said, "What we resist persists."

Smokey the Bear says, "Only you can prevent forest fires!" Likewise, only you can take the necessary actions to change anger patterns. We only change when we want to change. It's time to *"be doers of the Word and not hearers only."* (James 1:22) It's time to tap the powerful resources that God makes available to us so that we can learn *"to be angry and sin not."*(Ephesians 4:26-27)

"AN ANGER-CONTROL DRILL" MY PLAN TO SUCCEED

Step #1: THE CONFESSION STEP

I will acknowledge and accept the reality of my own sinful anger.
( )Yes ( )No

If we claim to be without sin, we deceive ourselves and the truth is not in us. If we confess our sins, he is faithful and just and will forgive us our sins and purify us from all unrighteousness. (1 John 1:8-9)

✞ I will honestly confess my sinful anger to God, to myself, and to others.

✞ No denial. No cover up. No excuses. No rationalizing. No lies.

✞ The statement, "He/She made me get angry," is a lie. I must now take responsibility for my anger. While I cannot control how others behave, I must learn to control myself. If I am practicing sinful anger, it is because I am choosing sinful anger.

✞ My anger is my responsibility and I will claim it.

✞ I will begin to view my sinful anger as a sin and label it as such.

✞ Related Scriptures: *Proverbs 29:22; Matthew 5:21-22; Ephesians 4:29-32*

"My Plan" For Taking "The Confession Step":

"God helping me, I will..."

Step #2: THE UNDERSTANDING STEP

Guided by God's Word, I will deepen and broaden my understanding as to how anger is affecting my life—constructively and destructively.
( )Yes ( )No

> *"All Scripture is God-breathed and is useful for teaching, rebuking, correcting, and training in righteousness, so that the man of God may be thoroughly equipped for every good work." ((2 Timothy 3:16-17)*

✞ Understand that anger is not always sinful. It can be a form of God-given energy that helps us to solve problems and stand for causes that are noble and right. It becomes sinful when it is exercised without proper restraints.

✞ Recognize your anger as a signal that something is not right—like the blinking red light on the dashboard of your car when there is a problem. This warning light must not be ignored! Take proper action to make the warning light go out.

✞ It is essential that you get to the bottom of your anger. In what is your sinful anger rooted? Such an examination is not an easy or painless task because, in many cases, the root of the problem may be within our own hearts. It is very difficult to be objective when it comes to an accurate self-analysis. The assistance of a trusted and informed friend or counselor is often necessary.

✞ Dig. Examine. Probe. Take a situation where you clearly practiced sinful anger and analyze it carefully. You must "get behind the anger" if you are to ever "get over it." Was there a legitimate injustice committed against you that needs to be confronted and resolved with the application of Christian principles? Could it be that you are bearing emotional trauma from your past that causes you to be overly sensitive and insecure? Are you using anger as a tool for getting your way? Do you need to be in control? Was your pride hurt or your security challenged? Is sinful jealousy and rivalry toward another person stirring anger within your heart? Is there someone you are unwilling to forgive—has bitterness filled your heart? Search for the actual taproot of your sinful anger. The real problem cannot be solved until the real problem is discovered. If necessary, you should seek the assistance of a capable Christian counselor.

✝ Related Scriptures: *Genesis 4:6-7; Psalm 42:5, 11; 43:5; Galatians 5:22-23; 1 John 3:11-16*

"My Plan" For Taking "The Understanding Step":

"God helping me, I will...

Step #3: THE PREVENTION STEP

God helping me, I will seek to prevent the fires of sinful anger from burning rather than struggling to extinguish them.
( )Yes ( )No

"Settle matters quickly with your adversary who is taking you to court." (Matthew 5:25)

✝ It's always better to prevent a fire than it is to extinguish one. Be alert! Be aware! As anger is being aroused, there is a critical period—sometimes very brief—when the spark of anger can be snuffed out by means of a satisfactory resolution. Watch for that "snuff point." At the first tinge of anger, exercise self-control. Small fires can become big fires very rapidly. Sparks of anger are much more manageable than an inferno of rage.

✝ Anger is a secondary emotion caused by other primary emotions. A primary emotion is what we feel first, and then comes anger. We may first feel hurt, cheated, disrespected, disregarded, accused, devalued, guilty, rejected, powerless, or trapped before we experience full-blown anger. Learn to recognize those "primary emotions" of impending anger and take preventive action quickly.

✝ If you don't fight anger early, it can quickly be fueled and fanned and blaze out of control. If possible, do not...do not...allow the spark of anger to burn. Prevention! Prevention! Prevention!

✝ Related Scriptures: *Proverbs 17:14; Matthew 5:23-26; Ephesians 4:26-27*

"My Plan" For Taking "The Prevention Step":

"God helping me, I will...

Step #4: THE RESTRAINT STEP

Being influenced by God's wisdom and love, I will learn to delay and restrain negative and hurtful expressions of anger.
( )Yes ( )No

"Be slow to get angry." (James 1:19)

✝ In situations that could be volatile, it is wise to allow time for prayer, study, personal reflection, and counsel with others. If possible, we must ask, "Do I have the facts? Have I heard both sides? What is the wise course?" Things may look differently once you have taken the time to back off and gain a broader perspective. Don't say the first thing that comes into your head. Keep your cool when you feel the temperature of anger rising.

✝ This approach to problem solving keeps us from speaking words that should not be spoken and behaving in ways that will bring grief, shame, and sin. Make sure that you are "acting in love" rather than "reacting in sinful anger."

✝ Angry people tend to jump to and act on conclusions that can be very inaccurate.

✝ Related Scriptures: *Proverbs 13:3, 20; 14:16-17; 15:22; 17:9, 14-15, 27-28; 18:2, 13, 17; 29:11; 20:3; Ephesians 4:26-27; James 1:19-20*

"My Plan" For Taking "The Restraint Step":

"God helping me, I will...

STEP #5: THE COMPASSION STEP

In the interest of practicing a healthy and holy anger, I will endeavor to show compassion by empathizing with others who may hurt or offend me.
( )Yes ( )No

> *"Father, forgive them, for they do not know what they are doing."*
> *(Luke 23:34)*

✝ Ask God to help you maintain sensitivity to the problems and struggles that may underlie the obnoxious actions of those who hurt you. A closed and bitter mind is a spawning ground for long-lasting anger issues. Be willing to see your own flaws and admit failure when you are convinced that such is warranted.

✝ Compassion does not excuse obnoxious behavior, but it may keep us from attacking the already weak or wounded person, which allows for emphasis on changing the undesired behavior.

✝ Do all within your power to resolve the troublesome matter as quickly as possible. Pray for a loving, forgiving spirit and resolve not to become trapped in lingering bitterness or grudge bearing. Pray for the ability to release sinful anger—to let it go!

✝ Related Scriptures: *Matthew 7:3-5; James 1:19; Galatians 6:1-2; Matthew 5:11-12, 25-26, 43-48; 18:21-35; Romans 12:17-21; Ephesians 4:26, 29-32*

"My Plan" For Taking "The Compassion Step":

"God helping me, I will…

STEP #6: THE CONFRONTATION STEP

When I have offended another person or when someone has hurt me, I will, in a spirit of love, confront the situation with a desire to promote healing and peace.
( )Yes ( )No

"Therefore, if you are offering your gift at the altar and there remember that your brother has something against you, leave your gift there in front of the altar. First go and be reconciled to your brother; then come and offer your gift. (Matthew 5:23-24)

"If your brother sins against you, go and show him his fault, just between the two of you. If he listens to you, you have won your brother over. But if he will not listen, take one or two others along, so that 'every matter may be established by the testimony of two or three witnesses.' If he refuses to listen to them, tell it to the church; and if he refuses to listen even to the church, treat him as you would a pagan or a tax collector. (Matthew 18:15-17)

✟ Whether you are the offender or the offended one, the right and healthy response is to communicate about the offense in the interest of promoting reconciliation and unity. Attack the problem, not the person. We must learn to express our anger in appropriate, non-destructive, and non-sinful ways.

✟ By venting our anger with the person or persons directly involved, we release emotional pressure and lessen the risk of an ugly display of sinful anger. Dealing with and sharing what is bothering you before it gets to that point are important. The goal must be to express anger in such a way so as to solve problems, not create bigger ones.

✝ Related Scriptures: *Galatians 6:1-2; Ephesians 4:25; Philippians 4:2-3*

"My Plan" For Taking "The Confrontation Step":

"God helping me, I will...

STEP #7: THE WARFARE STEP

My struggle is not against flesh and blood, but against the spiritual forces of evil in the heavenly realms.
( )Yes ( )No

> *"For our struggle is not against flesh and blood, but against the rulers, against the authorities, against the powers of this dark world and against the spiritual forces of evil in the heavenly realms."* (Ephesians 6:12)

✝ We must be fully aware that evil is not merely a "something"— behind the forces of evil is a "someone" who seeks to hurt and destroy us. In order to effectively combat sinful anger, we must learn to wage spiritual warfare. The enemy is real. The struggle is not easy. Yet, by the grace and power of God, we do have the means to overcome and win the battle with sinful anger. Equip yourself for spiritual warfare.

✞ Tap the power of prayer. God offers His power, but we must, in faith, tap that power supply. *(Matthew 6:13)* Pray this prayer and supply your own words of petition. *"My Father, I am a sinner. I am weak. I am now asking you to…"*

✞ When Jesus was tempted, He resisted Satan by using the *sword of the Holy Spirit*—Scripture. *(Ephesians 6:17)* In resisting temptation, Jesus boldly said to the devil, *"It is written…" (Matthew 4:1-11)* It worked for Jesus. It will work for you. You should have anger-related passages written on cards or marked in your Bible. Keep these close at hand. They are your weapons. Speak those words aloud when you are tempted to yield to the sin of anger.

✞ In our battle with the devil, we need a few trusted Christian friends who will encourage us, pray with us, or come to us in moments of struggle and crisis. You should share your struggle with one or two such mentors. Schedule time with them for prayer, study, and consultation. Stay closely connected to these people, sharing your victories and defeats.

✞ Recognize the importance of maintaining other spiritual disciplines that will help you to keep your heart *"set on the Holy Spirit"* and what he wants for your life. For example, be present when the church assembles, take advantage of small group Bible studies, pray with trusted friends, read and study your Bible regularly, and memorize and meditate on Scripture passages that are related to the control of anger.

✞ Related Scriptures: *Matthew 4:1-11; Matthew 5:23-24; 18:15-17; Ephesians 6:1-18; Galatians 6:1-2; James 5:18; I Peter 5:8-9*

"My Plan" For Taking "The Warfare Step":

"God helping me, I will…

STEP #8: THE FORGIVENESS STEP

Knowing how much God has forgiven me, I will learn to lavish forgiveness on those who have hurt me.
( )Yes ( )No

> *"Therefore, as God's chosen people, holy and dearly loved, clothe yourselves with compassion, kindness, humility, gentleness and patience. Bear with each other and forgive whatever grievances you may have against one another. Forgive as the Lord forgave you. And over all these virtues put on love, which binds them all together in perfect unity." (Colossians 3:12-14)*

✝ As we process anger, it is important to keep short accounts recognizing that harbored anger will fester and pour poison into your heart, mind, and body.

✝ Anger is a form of energy that tends to stir and activate evil motives and selfish thoughts. When we are angry, we tend to remember old offenses and previous mistakes from the past. Anger can turn poisonous quickly. Pema Chodron says, "Holding a grudge is like eating rat poison and expecting the rat to die." Forgiveness is the "Master's Key" to controlling sinful anger.

✝ Related Scriptures: *Matthew 5:38-48, 18:21-22; Ephesians 4:2-3, 26, 29-32; Colossians 3:12-14; James 1:19; 3:13-18; 1 Peter 3:8-12*

"My Plan" For Taking "The Forgiveness Step":

"God helping me, I will...

STEP #9: THE DEPENDENCY STEP

Knowing that I am weak and sinful, I will depend on the power that God supplies to control sinful anger.
( )Yes ( )No

"*I can do everything through him who gives me the strength.*" (Philippians 4:13)

✞ The strength for controlling anger comes from the Lord and the power of His Word.
✞ As believers, we are supernaturally equipped to be angry for the right reasons, at the right times, in the right ways, with the right people, with the right outcome. The Holy Spirit who lives within us helps us in these ways.
✞ Related Scriptures: *Romans 8:5-14; Philippians 1:15-21; 2 Timothy 4:14-18*

"My Plan" For Taking "The Dependency Step":

"God helping me, I will...

STEP #10: THE REDIRECTION STEP

Rather than allowing sinful anger to burn within me, I will seek to redirect that energy in the direction of some goal that is productive and constructive.
( )Yes ( )No

> *"Do not repay anyone evil for evil. Be careful to do what is right in the eyes of everybody. Do not be overcome by evil, but overcome evil with good. (Romans 12:17, 21)*

✞ This is not an easy decision. There must be a conscious decision to turn something harmful into something helpful. "Evil" spelled backward is "live." By the power of love, we can turn "evil" around and "live."

✞ In *Mark 3:1-5*, Jesus was angry with the religious leaders of His day, yet He redirected that anger and healed a man with a shriveled hand.

✞ Through the redirection of anger, we find creative ways to control the fires of anger. People are helped instead of hurt. God is honored instead of being dishonored.

✞ Related Scriptures: *Romans 12:14-21; 1 Peter 2:18-25*

"My Plan" For Taking "The Redirection Step":

"God helping me, I will...

STEP #11: THE MOVE ON STEP

Having shown a confessional, forgiving, and conciliatory spirit toward those with whom problems have existed, I will continue to show an attitude of love and move on in my Christian walk.
( )Yes ( )No

"If it is possible, as far as it depends on you, live at peace with everyone." (Romans 12:18)

✝ Once you have made a sincere effort to do what you can do to settle matters with others and extinguish the fires of anger, then you must "move on" and continue serving God without lingering guilt.
✝ Related Scriptures: *Acts 15:36-41; Romans 12:14-18*

"My Plan" For Taking "The Move On Step":

"God helping me, I will...

STEP #12: THE PERSEVERANCE STEP

As long as I have breath in my body, I will wage a battle against sinful anger.
( )Yes ( )No

"I eagerly expect and hope that I will in no way be ashamed, but will have sufficient courage so that now as always Christ will be exalted in my body, whether by life or by death. For to me, to live is Christ and to die is gain." (Philippians 1:20-21)

✝ Never give up! Someone said, "The Boston Marathon is run in April each year. The course is 26 miles, 285 yards long. About 2000 people sign up each year to run the endurance race. Not all finish. What defeats most that drop out is a hill about 6 miles from the finish line. It is called "heartbreak hill." Life has its "heartbreak hills." Run the race. Never quit.

✝ The boxer, Archie Moore, was once asked, "What's the key to being a champion?" His response: "Fight one more round." Persistence.

✝ Thomas Edison was unsuccessful in the first 96 experiments in his attempt to invent the light bulb. An assistant commented about all the failures. Edison's answer: "The work is not wasted. We now know 96 ways not to do it."

✝ The people who win the race of life are not those who never fall, stumble or tire. It's those who don't quit running. You must never, never quit fighting a battle against sinful anger!

✝ Related Scriptures: *1 Peter 5:8-11; Philippians 3:12-14*

"My Plan" For Taking "The Perseverance Step":

"God helping me, I will...